Religion in Focus

Islam

in today's world

Teacher's Resource Book

Religion in Focus
Islam
in today's world
Teacher's Resource Book

Claire Clinton
Sally Lynch
Janet Orchard
Deborah Weston
Angela Wright

John Murray

Other titles in this series:
Christianity in today's world Student's Book ISBN 0 7195 7193 6
Teacher's Resource Book ISBN 0 7195 7431 5
Judaism in today's world Student's Book ISBN 0 7195 7197 9
Teacher's Resource Book ISBN 0 7195 7433 1

Acknowledgements

The authors and publishers are grateful to the following for permission to include material in this book:

p.36 © Altair 1970; **p.95** Olaf Skarsholt.

While every effort has been made to contact copyright holders, the publishers apologise for any omissions, which they will be pleased to rectify at the earliest opportunity.

Examination questions are reproduced by kind permission of the Northern Examinations and Assessment Board (**pp.27, 49, 65** and **88**)

© Claire Clinton, Sally Lynch, Janet Orchard, Deborah Weston, Angela Wright 1999

First published 1999
by John Murray (Publishers) Ltd
50 Albemarle Street
London W1S 4BD

Reprinted 2001, 2002

All rights reserved. The material in this publication is copyright but permission is given to teachers to make copies of pages 9–10 and the worksheets for one-time use as instructional material within their own school (or other educational institution). This permission does not extend to the making of copies for use outside the institution in which they are made (e.g. in a resource centre), and the material may not be copied in unlimited quantities, kept on behalf of others, passed on or sold to third parties or stored for future use in a retrieval system. If you wish to use the material in any way other than as specified you must apply in writing to the publishers.

Layouts by Black Dog Design, Buckingham.
Illustrations by Oxford Illustrators Ltd.
Cover design by John Townson/Creation.
Typeset in 10/12pt Rockwell Light by Wearset Ltd, Boldon, Tyne and Wear.
Printed in Great Britain by Selwood Printing Ltd, West Sussex.

A CIP record for this publication is available from the British Library

ISBN 0 7195 7432 3
Student's Book ISBN 0 7195 7194 4

Contents

Unit titles	Page references to teacher's notes	Worksheet numbers
Unit 1: An Islamic world view	16	1.1–1.8
Unit 2: Thinking about Allah	29	2.1–2.18
Unit 3: Issues of life and death	52	3.1–3.13
Unit 4: Relationships	68	4.1–4.17
Unit 5: Global issues	91	5.1–5.24

Introduction

What is the value of Religious Education?

The authors of this book have all been involved with the development of GCSE RE over the last decade, particularly the short courses introduced in 1998. We believe that the short courses and full GCSEs which have emerged give RE a most valuable and exciting place in students' all-round education – they help make RE as relevant to all students today as it has ever been.

The practical importance of GCSE accreditation to the future of Key Stage 4 RE is obvious to all. What has been perhaps less emphasised is the opportunity opened up by the new courses to discover the deeper value of RE to the growth and development of the student.

A personal journey

One central aim of RE is to help students to see their way through the cloudy and difficult path that we call the journey of life. The 'way' may well be different for each person, but the best method of finding it is for our students to think for themselves about ultimate questions of meaning and value rather than to simply accept the values and beliefs of others.

It is this personal journey that can make RE so different from RS. RE is not just the academic study of phenomena associated with religions, it is a study which involves the students themselves, asking them to make a response to religious concepts, beliefs and values. On such a personal journey, to some extent, there are no right or wrong answers.

In-depth investigation

However, RE is more than a personal journey – it is also an in-depth investigation of a complex set of beliefs and values.

One aim of this course is to help students to see beyond the stereotypical Islam sometimes portrayed in the media (and even in RE lessons) which can too easily present an ill-informed or misleading account.

Through this course students investigate and respond to Muslim beliefs about moral and theological issues. Other books in the series investigate other world religions in a similar way.

The value of RE is increased greatly if students study a topic in depth. This produces higher-quality work from all students and an appropriate challenge for all abilities – it allows access to all, while also stretching the very highest attainers.

Thinking skills

John Scully, former Chief Executive of Apple Computers, has said: 'we should be preparing students for jobs of the future, jobs that will require thinking skills, not rote memorisation and repetition'. Yet current educational research suggests that only about 20 per cent of our GCSE level students can use complex thinking skills. The 80 per cent majority are poor at empathising; they jump to conclusions; have difficulty with abstract or generalised solutions to problems; can't accept that there may be more than one answer to a problem; they see their lives and the world around them in black and white rather than in shades of grey. The risk is that the time pressures of the prescribed curriculum deepen this problem early in the school, turning students into surface learners.

The GCSE years are a key time to make this transition to higher-order thinking skills. And RE is a good vehicle through which to do it. In this course, particularly in studying the issues of morality and in the philosophy and theology, students learn to generalise; abstract; analyse; classify; contrast; reframe ideas and communicate conclusions in a wide variety of contexts. RE requires work with concepts which no other subject on the curriculum demands.

RE also develops understanding of people. The skills required for exploring other people's values and beliefs make short course RE not only an intellectually challenging subject but also an intensely relevant one to the current world in which emotional intelligence, the ability to empathise and to understand different points of view, is a vital ingredient of success in a wide range of careers.

Clarification of values

The current time is also a ripe one in which to be helping students to reflect for themselves, to weigh up issues and to consider what is important in life. The world that students are in the process of inheriting is vastly different from that of their teachers' and parents' generation. With an increased emphasis on personal choice and its associated personal accountability, the importance of values to guide students' decisions which affect their own or others' lives has never been greater.

INTRODUCTION

The aims of *Religion in Focus: Islam in today's world*

To explore fundamental questions which are immediately interesting and relevant to the student.

As teachers we know how difficult it is to motivate and capture the interest of students at KS4. ***Religion in Focus*** aims to start 'where they are at' and to raise issues that young people want to talk about. We have found in our discussions with colleagues in all types of school that the fundamental questions in the new RE syllabuses are just the sort of things that young people want to discuss. This course allows them space to consider these issues – and hopefully to get a GCSE grade out of it too!

To study selected aspects of a religion in depth rather than attempting a superficial survey.

As teachers we feel strongly that students should have sufficient information, in sufficient detail, in order to study issues from a religious perspective in an informed and mature way. We have therefore attempted to give some detail and a wide variety of sources of authority in dealing with religious teachings about each issue. This course allows students to follow a GCSE RE syllabus in depth. It presents a wide variety of Muslim viewpoints, teaching on and responses to fundamental questions of life, and moral issues. It allows students to explore in-depth *why* Muslims have a variety of responses to issues. It enables reasoned reflection and clear thinking about issues affecting Muslims.

To meet the requirements of the National Criteria The National Criteria for GCSE short course RE describe the aims of RE as follows. The students should:

- *acquire and develop knowledge and develop understanding of the beliefs, values and traditions of one or more religions;*
- *consider the influence of the beliefs, values and traditions associated with one or more religions;*
- *consider religious and other responses to moral issues;*
- *identify, investigate and respond to fundamental questions of life raised by religion and human experience.*

To highlight different viewpoints held by different traditions within a religion.

All GCSE RE specifications require students to be able to answer questions from the viewpoint of more than one religion, or more than one perspective within a religion. Even more important than this, we believe that it is vital for young people to be presented with a wide variety of opinions on and responses to issues, so that they can seek guidance in formulating their own responses and support in upholding them.

Teachers preparing students for GCSE may use this book in conjunction with either *Christianity in today's world* or *Judaism in today's world* to allow a very wide breadth of response in the examination.

To encourage a personal response from the student but one which is considered and informed by their study of a religion. Facilitating this personal response is the key objective of this series.

Whilst gaining a good grade at GCSE must be a prime aim for all students, there is far more to education than that. The three steps in each investigation – the issue raiser, the in-depth information and the exploration of responses – allow students to engage with the material and encourage them to make their own, reasoned response. Some investigations will be immediately more attractive to each student than others. Yet in order to be 'religiously educated' young people need to study and to be able to formulate, articulate and justify their own views on a wide range of issues; the material that this course provides will encourage that.

INTRODUCTION

Structure of the Student's Book

Unit 1 introduces concepts dealt with by the rest of the course.

1.1 and 1.3 examine the basic beliefs of Islam and how they guide Muslims in making moral decisions.

1.2 explores various sources of authority for Muslims as they make decisions.

1.4 investigates the life and work of Muslims today.

Unit 2 deals with theology.

Units 3–5 deal with moral issues, particularly those required for study in the principal short course syllabuses.

Unit 1: An Islamic world view
1.1 THE OPENING: What does Al-Fatihah mean to Muslims?
1.2 SOURCES OF MORAL AUTHORITY: How do Muslims find out how Allah wants them to live?
1.3 IMAN AND IBADAH: Islam is . . .
1.4 DIVERSITY IN ISLAM: Who are the Muslims?
1.5 THE INDIVIDUAL IN SOCIETY: How can individual Muslims change the world around them?

Unit 2: Thinking about Allah
2.1 THE NATURE OF ALLAH: The One and Only . . .
2.2 HOW GOD MAY BE KNOWN: How is Allah revealed to human beings?
2.3 SUFFERING AND EVIL: Why is suffering part of Allah's plan?
Review tasks

Unit 3: Issues of life and death
3.1 INTRODUCTION: What do Muslims believe about life and death?
3.2 ABORTION: Can abortion ever be justified?
3.3 EUTHANASIA: Why is euthanasia forbidden in Islam?
3.4 CAPITAL PUNISHMENT: Is it ever right to kill a human being as a punishment?
Review tasks

Unit 4: Relationships
4.1 INTRODUCTION: Ummah – the caring community
4.2 SEX, MARRIAGE AND DIVORCE: Why do Muslims say people should marry?
4.3 EQUALITY: Does Islam truly liberate women?
4.4 PREJUDICE AND DISCRIMINATION: How do Muslims respond to racism?
Review tasks

Unit 5: Global issues
5.1 WEALTH AND POVERTY: How should Muslims use their money?
5.2 THE ENVIRONMENT: Live in this world as if you were going to live forever!
5.3 WAR AND PEACE: Is it ever right to fight?
Review tasks

Each unit contains a number of in-depth investigations which vary in length according to the complexity of the content. See opposite for the features of each investigation.

INTRODUCTION

Features of an investigation

Title
The title is usually in the form of a question to be investigated. The question itself can be opened up for classroom discussion before you plough into the unit.

Sources
A wide variety of pictures, drawings and real quotations are used in various ways:

- to convey the teaching of various sources of authority
- to highlight divergent opinions within Islam
- to stimulate students' thinking about an issue
- to humanise the study.

These Sources are the raw material of the course. They are not optional extras. All Sources are used in some way, either in tasks or in questions.

Checkpoints
These information boxes provide background information, or explain key words or concepts which students must know for the examination.

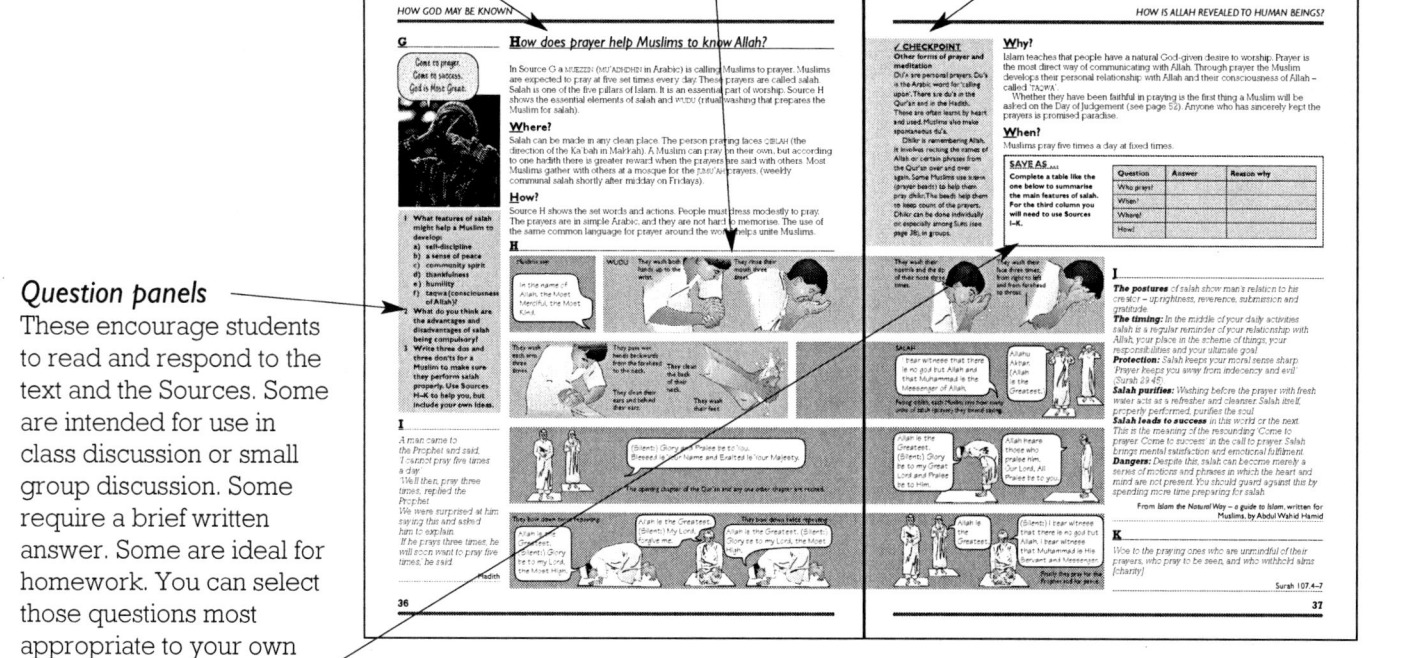

Question panels
These encourage students to read and respond to the text and the Sources. Some are intended for use in class discussion or small group discussion. Some require a brief written answer. Some are ideal for homework. You can select those questions most appropriate to your own plan of work.

Boxed tasks
These are the main building blocks of the classroom investigation. There are different approaches which allow for differentiation and variety. The purpose of each one is outlined in the detailed teacher's notes. The distinction between the different types of tasks is not rigid but these are the four main categories we have used:

ACTIVITY These may be research-based writing tasks or discussion-style, but they have in common that they require students **to engage creatively or imaginatively** with the material.

DISCUSS These are similar to the questions but are more central to the development of the investigation.

SAVE AS ... These tasks are designed to help students **to get information into their notebooks** or onto paper for future revision. Often they appear at the end of an activity, allowing the learning that has taken place in the activity to be transferred onto paper.

FOCUS TASK In terms of syllabus coverage and assessment of students' overall grasp of the topics, the Focus Tasks are some of the most important tasks. There is one Focus Task for each key topic in the main specifications.

They vary in style from examination-style questions to creative assignments. What they have in common is that they are **summative** tasks which bring together a wide range of learning and insight. They focus on particularly important issues or sum up key ideas from the investigation. Some of them range across a whole unit or bring together ideas from a whole term's work.

Think of them as **the review points** on your journey through the investigation. In the same way as the 'Save As . . .' tasks, they also generate a written response which can be used for revision. There are often worksheets in this Teacher's Resource Book to support the most important tasks, or the 'recording' stages of the tasks.

Islam in today's world Teacher's Resource Book

How does Islam in today's world cover the content of GCSE short and full course syllabuses from examination 2003?

Islam in today's world	AQA (B) (1) Thinking about God and morality	AQA (B) (2) Key beliefs, ultimate questions and life issues	AQA (B) (3) Faith studies and ethics in two religions	AQA (B) (4) Truth, spirituality and contemporary issues	AQA (C) World religions – Islam	EDEXCEL (A)	OCR (A) World religions – Islam	OCR (B) Philosophy and ethics	WJEC (A) Islam	WJEC (B)
✓ = total coverage	✓							✓		✓
Scheme of assessment	Full: choose one from 1–3 and do 4. Short: choose one from 1–4. Any one, two or three religions can form the basis of student answers				With reference to one religion (short) or two religions (full), selected from the six principal religions in the UK. Complete one piece of coursework (short) and two pieces of coursework (full)	Full: one unit from Module 1 (A–G) and one from Module 2 (H–P). Short: any one unit	Full: take two 90 minute papers plus either coursework or Paper 11. Short: take two 60 minute papers	Full: either Papers 1 and 2 or Papers 3 and 4, plus coursework. Short: one paper plus coursework. Full course: eight units from the ten. Short course: any four units	Full: two papers and two pieces of coursework. Short: one paper and one piece of coursework	Full: two papers (A+B) and two pieces of coursework or two (longer) papers. Half this requirement
Unit 1: An Islamic world view	Thinking about morality – ways of making moral decisions; the individual in society	A: Key beliefs – the significance of Muhammad; nature and the significance of the Qur'an		a) The nature of spirituality. Religious authorities. Sacred writings	Beliefs and sources of authority: Qur'an, Sunnah, Muhammad, Shari'ah, Sunni and Shi'ah	K: Community and Tradition – Qur'an, Muhammad, Sunni and Shi'ah. Living the Muslim life: Shari'ah, Halal and Haram	Beliefs: Muhammad, 5 Pillars. Major divisions and interpretations: Sunni and Shi'ah, variety of practice	The Nature of God: The authority of the Qur'an; the nature of belief; Shirk. Good and evil: Shaytan/Iblis	Sources of Authority: Qur'an, Muhammad, Shari'ah. Morality. Lifestyle and social practice: ihsan	A2: Is it fair?: Shari'ah. A3: Looking for meaning
Unit 2: Thinking about Allah	Thinking about God – the existence of God; suffering and evil; the design of the universe; religious experience. The nature of God – personal, impersonal, transcendent, immanent, one or many; general and special revelation	A: Key beliefs – the significance of Muhammad; nature and the significance of the Qur'an; the attributes of Allah (Surah 1, 112); Tawhid; The Five Pillars of Islam; Shahadah. B: Questions of meaning – arguments for and against belief in God	A: Public and private worship. Salah, including times; the call to prayer; ablutions (wudu), prayer sequence (rak'ah). The importance of Jumu'ah (Friday prayer). The use of aids to worship. The role of the imam and mu'adhin (muezzin). The importance of the Qur'an. Prayer and study of the Qur'an in the home	a) The nature of spirituality. b) Claims to truth • religious • authorities • sacred writings • conscience. c) Some ways of expressing spirituality in society: • individual • commitment	Beliefs and sources of authority: Tawhid, Risalah, Qur'an, Sunnah, Muhammad. Practice and organisation: 5 pillars: Shahadah, salah	A, D: Believing in Allah: the nature of Allah; religious experience; salah; evil and suffering. K: Beliefs and values: • tawhid • risalah • al-Qadr. Community and tradition – Muhammad. Worship and celebration: Shahadah, salah	Beliefs: God, Muhammad, 5 Pillars – Shahadah, salah. Festivals, fasts and special days: Jumu'ah. Places and forms of worship: salah and du'a	The nature of God: teaching of Muhammad; the authority of the nature of belief; prayer in mosque and home; Tawhid. Religion and science: Good and evil: Allah, Qur'an, conscience, prayer, submission. Religion and equality: conversion, forgiveness	Worship: setting, preparation, form. Sources of Authority: Muhammad. Beliefs: Allah, Risalah, Shahadah. Community: global. Morality: free will. Lifestyle and social practice: ihsan. Identity and belonging: Salah	A3: Looking for meaning: Tawhid, 99 names. A4: Identity and belonging: Al-Qadr and free will. B4: Authority – religion and state: Qur'an, Shari'ah. B5: Suffering and evil: Allah and his attributes, Shaytan, al-Qadr, Salah, Muhammad
Unit 3: Issues of life and death	Thinking about morality – making moral decision: absolute and relative: the relationship between belief and behaviour; human rights and responsibilities: • abortion	A: Key beliefs – the nature and significance of the Qur'an: The Day of Judgement, Akhirah, Heaven and Hell. B: Questions of meaning: life after death. C: Life issues –abortion		b) Religious attitudes to matters of death: euthanasia, suicide. Religious attitudes to crime and punishment	Beliefs and sources of authority: Akhirah, Qur'an. Practice and organisation: rites of passage. Relevance and application: Matters of life and death	A, D: Matters of life and death: • akhirah • sanctity of life • abortion • euthanasia. K: Beliefs and values: • shirk, akhirah. Living the Muslim life: • death rituals	Beliefs: Day of Judgement, life after death. Religion in the Community and the family: funeral rites. Sacred writings: the Qur'an and sunnah	Death and the Afterlife: body and soul, life after death, funeral rites. Religion and medical ethics: abortion, euthanasia, suicide. Religion, peace and justice: criminals, social justice	Celebration: death. Sources of Authority: Qur'an. Beliefs: Akhirah	A2: Is it fair?: justice. A3: Looking for meaning: life is sacred, suicide and euthanasia; life after death; akhirah: heaven and hell. B2: Religion and medicine: life as a gift, Allah decides, abortion. B3: Religious expression:

						leading others to faith **B4:** Authority – religion and state: Qur'an, Shari'ah **B5:** Suffering and evil; Allah and his attributes, Shaytan, judgement, heaven and hell
Unit 4: Relationships	**Thinking about morality** – human rights and responsibilities: • sex • marriage • divorce • prejudice and discrimination	**A: Key beliefs** – the significance of Muhammad **C: Life issues** – religion and prejudice	**A:** Places of worship: **B:** Relationships Rights and responsibilities: a) Human sexuality and sexual relationships b) Married and family life c) Issues in human relationships d) Prejudice and discrimination in society	Beliefs and sources of authority: Ummah Practice and organisation: Mosque Rites of passage Relevance and application: Ummah Family relationships Justice and equality	c) Some ways of expressing spirituality in society: • membership of a faith community		**A, D:** Believing in Allah: religious upbringing Matters of life and death: Contraception Marriage and the family: marriage, sex, divorce, the family Social Harmony: role of men and women prejudice and discrimination Ummah hajj **K:** Living the Muslim life: Hijab Birth The Mosque	**Beliefs:** Muhammad **Places and forms of worship:** the Mosque, imam **Religion in the Community and the family:** birth, nurture, marriage, role of family	**The nature of belief:** Mosque **Religion and human relationships:** men and women; marriage; divorce; sex and contraception **Religion and equality:** Qur'an; racism; women	Celebration: birth, marriage Community: Mosque, muezzin, imam Morality: family, marriage, divorce, sex, contraception, prejudice, discrimination Lifestyle and social practices: dress	**A1:** Relationships: sex; marriage – arranged, polygamy, divorce **A2:** Is it fair?: racial equality; Ummah; women's rights **A4:** Identity and belonging: Ummah, birth, children **B3:** Religious expression: Mosques **B4:** Authority – religion and state: justice, mercy, capital punishment
Unit 5: Global issues	**Thinking about morality** – global issues: • world poverty • war and peace • the natural world	**A: Key beliefs** – The significance of Muhammad; The Five Pillars: zakah **C: Life issues** – war and peace **D:** Planet Earth: the care of the planet	e) Animals and the environment	Beliefs and sources of authority: Jihad Practice and organisation: 5 pillars Zakah Relevance and application: Sadaqah respect and concern for the created world	c) Some ways of expressing spirituality in society: • support for voluntary organisations • Religious attitudes to rich and poor in society		**A, D:** Believing in Allah: zakah Religion wealth and poverty **K:** Beliefs and values: khalifah Worship and celebration: zakah Living the Muslim life: jihad	**Beliefs:** Muhammad, 5 Pillars – zakah, jihad **Religion in the Community and the family:** zakah	**Religion and science:** environmental issues **Religion, poverty and wealth:** causes; use of money; charity **Religion, peace and justice:** jihad: violence; pacifism	Celebration: zakah Morality: jihad, poverty Lifestyle and social practices: jihad, sadaqah, greeting	**A2:** Is it fair?: zakah and sadaqah, work of an organisation **A5:** Our world: creation, khalifahs, animals, responsibility and the Ummah **B1:** Religion and conflict: jihad, mercy and peace, example of Muhammad **B5:** Suffering and evil; zakah

Islam in today's world Teacher's Resource Book

INTRODUCTION

Planning your course

It is possible to work through the Student's Book as it stands, as a course in its own right. It is also possible to use it flexibly within a course of your own design.

Whichever route you choose, there is clearly a lot more in the book than most schools will need. This is deliberate, to give you flexibility and choice – so planning is essential.

Stage 1: overall course structure

We would suggest that before you begin teaching students about how Muslims might respond to different moral issues, you tackle the ideas in Units 1 and 2. These two units establish the important general concepts which underpin moral decision-making in Islam.

Next use the chart on page 6 to select the sections of Units 3–5 that apply to your syllabus. The book is structured around NEAB Syllabus D but is suited to most other syllabuses.

Units 3–5 may be tackled in any order although you may find that you need to investigate Unit 3.1 first, if you want students to understand that the Muslim 'long-term view' has an impact on all moral issues.

Stage 2: detailed course planning

For more detailed planning the chart on the next page will help you.

In column 1 note down the investigations you intend to tackle, in the order in which you intend to tackle them.

In column 2 note how long you intend to give to each investigation.

In column 3 select tasks that suit the needs of your class. There are many more tasks and questions than most classes will need. This allows for choice and differentiation, given the very varying time allowed for RE in different schools and given the range of abilities being taught in a typical RE class.

In column 4 note ideas for differentiation. The written material in the Student's Book is suited to average or slightly above average students. The pictorial sources and tasks should be accessible to all students. Some students may need support in dealing with the written material in order to perform the tasks. The teacher's notes and worksheets give a wide variety of support material for all abilities.

In column 5 note additional resources: videos, magazines, ICT, etc., which might be needed. As well as commercially produced material, you should ideally already have your own collections of newspaper cuttings, videos of useful TV programmes, tapes of radio programmes, pictures and postcards to stimulate discussion. All of these things can then be added to the resources provided by the course.

Detailed teaching notes

This Teacher's Resource Book provides detailed notes for the use of the investigations in the Student's Book. The notes explain some of the reasoning behind the course design, and suggest ways of using the tasks as well as other approaches or resources which you could try out.

Photocopiable worksheets

A set of photocopiable worksheets for each unit follows the teaching notes on that unit. The intended use of the worksheets is explained in the notes.

The worksheets serve a wide variety of purposes:

- **Time savers** Some of the more complex grids, tables and sources are reproduced in photocopiable form to reduce the time needed to prepare for an activity; for example: Worksheet 5.9.
- **Support material for the less able** Writing frames, cloze exercises, cut and paste activities are good support for less able students; for example: Worksheet 2.6.
- **Homework** Many of the sheets are suitable for homework; for example: Worksheets 2.1 and 5.1.
- **Debate and discussion slips** Some sheets provide pre-prepared statements/viewpoints to encourage widespread and balanced discussion; for example: Worksheet 3.10.
- **Qur'an 'file cards'** These provide at a glance references to useful passages that students should learn to include in their answers; for example: Worksheet 2.17.
- **End of unit tests** These are in the form of a quick quiz to enable students to find out what they have learned and what they need to know; for example: Worksheet 1.8.
- **Examination practice** For each unit there are examination questions which can be used as classroom tasks, homework, examination practice or summary exercises. For example: Worksheet 1.7.

Other planning issues

Some other issues will also affect your general and detailed planning.

Local Agreed Syllabuses

Many Local Agreed Syllabuses simply state that a school is complying with the syllabus for Key Stage 4 if it follows an approved GCSE syllabus in RE or RS. Some, however, have more specific demands and, although we believe that this series will enable teachers to cover the requirements of most Agreed Syllabuses in enabling students to learn both from and about religion, it is not possible for us to be sure we have provided for the distinctive needs of all Local Agreed Syllabuses, so check your syllabus carefully.

GCSE *Short Course RE Planning Sheet*

Syllabus and options followed: _____
Time available: Year 10 _____ Year 11 _____

1: Investigation headings	2: Time to be given	3: Tasks to be used	4: Differentiation techniques to be used	5: Additional resources needed

Scheme of Work for GCSE Short Course Religious Studies

Topic from the Syllabus: _____   Time to be given: _____

Learning experiences, in relation to each assessment objective	Key concepts and vocabulary specified	Written resources available	Additional resources available to support	Audio-visual aids

INTRODUCTION

Additional resources

The GCSE short course was designed to be up to date and relevant to the interests of Key Stage 4 students. Teachers need to keep up to date too, by following developments at home and abroad on issues such as euthanasia, marriage and divorce, abortion and so on. One way of doing this is to appoint some students as research assistants who will collect cuttings and other items for the whole group's use, as well as their own. There are a number of TV series which are worth checking out and taping for use in the classroom (this is quite legal for classroom use). Series such as *Heart of the Matter*, *Everyman*, *Inside Story* and *Cutting Edge* quite often deal with moral issues from a variety of points of view, and occasionally specifically from a Muslim viewpoint. For the past few years, the BBC has put out a series of programmes about Islam during the month of Ramadan. They are usually transmitted late at night, so set your video timer! Both the BBC and Independent Television have also recently brought out new collections of RE material which can be bought and/or taped. The BBC's RE Collection and *Taking Issue* and *Belief File* are worth looking at.

Charities and Muslim organisations are another good source of information. These provide information about their own work and may also sell videos and other resources; many have education departments. Teachers must remember that these are charities and may expect a donation; also that they are more likely to be helpful if one student writes on behalf of the whole group rather than all sending begging letters. Some of the material will also be biased to the viewpoint of the charity, naturally, and so care should be taken when using it.

A list of useful addresses of charities and organisations is provided on pages 14–15. This could be given to students, but its primary use is to help the teacher in locating additional resources from the original sources.

Information and communication technology

ICT is increasingly valuable in RE. It has had a slow start but there is now some useful software for RE, and not all specifically from RE publishers.

ICT can add variety to teaching styles, but there are drawbacks. There is the danger of students taking too long over work and 'experimenting' with the technology rather than really working at RE. Teachers must also guard against the temptation for students to plagiarise material from electronic sources and pass it off as their own work. However, these problems can be eradicated with careful planning and supervision.

There is an obvious place in RE for using commercially available software or the Internet to widen your resource base in research, particularly for reference material. CD-Roms exist such as *Aspects of Religion* (Nelson). The *Guardian* CD-Rom is a useful tool for researching issues from newspapers, and electronic encyclopaedias are helpful in finding definitions and legal material. Lat Blaylock at the Christian Education Movement (Royal Buildings, Victoria Street, Derby DE1 1GW, 01332 296655) has compiled a useful list of addresses on the World Wide Web, and CEM also has a publication about ICT and RE.

There is an amazing amount of material specifically about Islam on the Internet, but be aware that material can vary wildly in quality and value, and some is very offensive indeed! We have identified good sources at various points. A good place to start in searching the Web on any aspect of RE, including Islam, is the RE-XS site hosted by the University College of St Martin in Lancaster. A second general RE site is the RESite (see address list on page 15).

Other useful sites for Islam are those that specialise in stories, calligraphy, personal accounts of people who have reverted to Islam, the Qur'an and the Hadith. See the address list for further details. You may find ways of using the material in this book that we had not intended or even thought of. If you develop good teaching ideas which you would like to share with others, then the 'teacher's cupboard' on the RE-XS site allows you to do so. The address is: re-xs.ucsm.ac.uk/schools.

Wordprocessing and desktop publishing can of course improve the presentation of students' work (for example, Worksheet 3.7) as can clipart. Students can be helped to identify what illustration is appropriate for the context.

Wordprocessing can also help in students' conceptual grasp of issues. The work undertaken by the NCET-sponsored project on ICT in History, regarding the role of wordprocessing in helping develop students' thinking skills and organisational skills, is well worth looking at for cross-curricular implications.

The examination

Many of the tasks in the Student's Book are designed to enable students to record information in some form. How this is done – books or folders, or whatever – is left to the teacher to decide. This is the students' written record to return to when they come to revise for the examination. By writing down or recording information in some way students should be internalising it more thoroughly and thus learning more.

However, the need to record in a revisable form is sometimes at odds with making an activity interesting and engaging. So on occasions we have given students more help by bringing out the main learning points they will need to remember. The 'Save As . . .' tasks have already been mentioned, as has the role of Focus Tasks in creating a revisable record.

This Resource Book has end of unit quizzes for all units. These are designed to ease students' recall of content they will need for the exam.

We have included exam-style questions as review tasks at the end of each unit in the Student's Book, and examination practice worksheets in this Resource Book.

INTRODUCTION

Ensure you also use questions from your own examination if we have not included examples.

As the new specifications mature, Chief Examiners and Examination Boards will develop their question papers in the light of responses each year from candidates and their teachers. Examination Boards always find such responses after the exam useful. The teaching unions have response forms which may be sent, or a simple letter will suffice.

Coursework

It is possible to tackle GCSE RE without doing coursework, but there are some specifications which offer it as an option. Many tasks in the Student's Book can be adapted as coursework tasks. Students should be encouraged to use, but not to plagiarise, the book as a source for their coursework. The teacher's notes in this Resource Book give advice about additional sources of information.

Supporting non-specialist teachers

In the majority of schools RE is taught by a combination of specialists and non-specialists, and it is important that the specialists offer the non-specialists support. We have attempted to provide material to stimulate the students and the teachers alike but you will need to monitor carefully the effectiveness of the tasks you have chosen, and to compare classroom experiences with other teachers. It is vital to plan well for lessons by reading material in advance and gathering any extra resources such as videos or newspapers and other source materials.

Using the faith community

As we have already emphasised, Islam is about real life. It is practised by real people in the real world. It is often hard for children who have never met members of a faith not to see their practices as strange or to appreciate that their beliefs are sincerely held. We have tried in this book to introduce students to as many modern Muslims as possible, particularly those living in Britain today. This of course can be no substitute for meeting Muslims 'in the flesh', so we would urge you to use any opportunities you have to achieve this. In Britain's major cities there will be many opportunities easily available. Outside the major cities, you may be surprised to find 'Islamic societies' listed in local library directories, or clubs and societies or mosques listed in the 'Places of worship' section of the Yellow Pages. Another useful publication is the *Muslim Directory*, which lists many mosques and Muslim organisations in the country (see the address list for further details).

It may be that you have staff who are Muslims, but do not assume that just because someone has a Muslim name, they are an expert on how you apply the Shari'ah law to euthanasia, for example!

Ways of using visitors from faith communities in RE lessons
- Interview the visitors.
- Set up a panel with visitors from different denominations or traditions to respond to questions or debate issues. This could aim to highlight denominational differences, or similarities.
- Invite visitors to discuss with students one-to-one or one-to-two.
- Invite visitors to give talks about specific issues.
- Invite visitors to describe their sources of authority on a moral issue.
- Invite visitors to lead a workshop or seminar on a specific issue.
- Invite them to work with a small group of more, or less, able students.

Guidelines on using members of faith communities
- Always talk to visitors first and ensure that they are suited to working with students. Can they speak at the right level?
- Ensure that visitors understand why they are involved. For example, ensure that they know they are not there to convert students.
- Prepare your students. Advise them about appropriate behaviour, responses and courtesy.
- Prepare your resources and questions etc. well in advance of the lesson.
- Be hospitable. Arrange for students to meet visitors and provide hospitality if possible. Check dietary requirements in advance.
- Ensure that visitors know a bit about your course and syllabus, what you have covered and are about to cover, and their place in it.
- Confirm all arrangements in writing.
- Be sensitive to the visitor – might they have difficulties if confronted with others of different views (including the students)?
- Express your gratitude. Get students to write to thank the visitors. One of our schools ran a competition for students to produce their own 'thank you' cards to be used to write to thank RE visitors.

Using real people from the faith communities presents many opportunities, but also a few pitfalls which need to be avoided. The Christian Education Movement has produced an excellent booklet which will help you make the most of visitors, and visits too (see page 11).

Using your students as a resource

Some of the Sources in the Student's Book may raise controversy. A Muslim reading the view of a particular Muslim may not agree and may or may not want to explain why. This will be a timely reminder that the students in your class are your richest teaching resource when they are part of the faith community you are investigating, and could greatly enhance the discussion.

INTRODUCTION

This opportunity has a caveat attached. Care will need to be taken throughout the course, that students who are members of faith communities are not offended either by attitudes with which they could never agree, or by comments made by other students.

Muslims in your class may have knowledge or opinions to share, but they should never be set up as the expert or asked to respond as a Muslim when they did not volunteer to do so.

Addresses

Organisations and charities

Amana Trust
PO Box 2842
London W6 9ZH
0181 748 2424
Fax: 0181 846 9797

An-Nisa Society (Families Group)
Bestways Complex
2 Abbey Road
London NW10 7UL
0181 838 0311

Commission for Racial Equality
Elliot House
10–12 Allington Street
London SE1E 5EH
0171 828 7022
Fax: 0171 630 7605
Website: www.cre.gov.uk

Imam Khoei Islamic Centre (Shi'a Muslims)
Chevening Road
London NW6 6TN
0171 372 7706

Iqra Trust
24 Culross Street
London W1Y 3HE
0171 493 1572
Fax: 0171 493 7899

Islamic Awareness and Education Project
(Support for Teachers)
PO Box 1175
Swindon SN4 9RS
01793 511520
Fax: 01793 513002
Website: www.islam-for-beginners.com

Islamic Foundation
Markfield Conference Centre
Ratby Lane
Markfield LE67 9SY
01530 244944
Fax: 01530 244946
Website: http://dialspace.dial.pipex.com/town/street/gbg00/index.html

Islamic Foundation for Ecology and Environmental Sciences (IFEES)
PO Box 5051
Birmingham B20 3RZ
0121 440 3500
Fax: 0121 440 8144

Q-News
Dexion House
2–4 Empire Way
Wembley
Middlesex HA9 0XA
0181 903 0819
Fax: 0181 903 0820

Islamic Computing Centre
73 St Thomas Road
London N4 2QJ

Islamic Relief
151b Park Road
London NW8 7WW
0171 722 0039
Fax: 0171 722 3228
Website: www.islamic-relief.org.uk

Islamic Shari'a Council
34 Francis Road
London E10 6PW
Tel/Fax: 0181 558 0581

Islamica Magazine
Islamic Society
London School of Economics
Houghton Street
London WC2A 2AE
Fax: 01530 244946

Mountain of Light (publications by Yusuf Islam and others)
PO Box 7404
London N7 8JQ
0171 700 7586
Fax: 0171 700 0425

Muslim Aid
PO Box 3
London N7 8LR
0171 609 4425
Fax: 0171 609 4943
Website: www.muslimaid.org.uk

Muslim College/Muslim Law Shari'a Council
20 Creffield Road
London W5 3RP
0181 992 6636
Fax: 0181 993 3946

ADDRESSES

Muslim Directory
65a Grosvenor Road
London W7 1HR
0181 840 0020
Fax: 0181 840 8819
Website: www.muslimdirectory.co.uk

Muslim Educational Trust (support and publications for teachers and pupils)
130 Stroud Green Road
London N4 3RZ
0171 272 8502
Fax: 0171 281 3457

Muslim News
PO Box 380
Harrow
Middlesex HA2 6LL
0171 836 8988
Fax: 0171 836 8870

Muslim Women's Helpline
11 Main Drive
GEC East Lane Estate
Wembley
Middlesex HA9 7PX
Tel: ADMIN 0181 908 3205
Tel: 0181 904 8193/0181 908 6715
Website: http://amrnet.demon.co.uk/related/mwhl.html

Muslim World League (General Information)
46 Goodge Street
London W1P 1FJ
0171 636 7568
Fax: 0171 637 5034

REsite (website)
www.theresite.org.uk

Re-XS (website)
http://re-xs.ucsm.ac.uk/schools/

Runnymede Trust (published report on Islamophobia)
134 Aldersgate Street
London EC1A 4JA
0171 600 9666
Fax: 0171 600 8529

Sound Vision
37B New Cavendish Street
London W1M 8JR

Trends Magazine
PO Box 18729
London E6 3UR
07000 968646

UK Islamic Mission
202 North Gower Street
London NW1 2LY
0171 387 2157
Fax: 0171 383 0867

World Federation of Khoja Shia Ithna-Asheri Muslim Communities
Islamic Centre
Wood Lane
Stanmore
Middlesex HA7 4JB
0181 954 9881
Fax: 0181 954 9034
Website: www.world-federation.org

UNIT 1

An Islamic world view

Overview

This introductory unit establishes some basic ideas:

- the core beliefs of Islam (1.1) and (1.3)
- that Islam is a religion that is a way of life (1.1)
- sources of moral authority (1.2)
- the link between religious beliefs, values and behaviour (1.3)
- diversity within Islam (1.4)
- jihad, as the challenge of doing what is right and good (1.5).

Starting strategies

Students may or may not have studied aspects of Islam as part of the locally agreed Syllabus for RE at Key Stage 3. It goes without saying that you start from what they already know. For some, Unit 1 may be more of a re-cap, while for others it will be new territory.

One issue to be confronted head-on is 'stereotypes'. As you will see from investigation 4.4, images of Islam in the media, and in popular perception, are sometimes extremely ill-informed and possibly downright antagonistic. The 'Islamophobia' report (see pages 90–91) talked of this as a closed view of Islam, and it is all too common among students and teachers. You might choose to confront stereotypes much earlier on in the course than we have done. Certainly you might wish to begin the course by setting up an ongoing research bank of cuttings/articles about Islam (see pages 4 and 89).

1.1 What does Al-Fatihah mean to Muslims?

Over these four pages, students are introduced to the core beliefs of Islam through the words of Al-Fatihah, the opening surah (division) of the Qur'an. It is important to emphasise how familiar these words are to all Muslims because they recite them every time they pray. **Worksheet 1.1** will help students to focus on what the words mean to the two Muslims featured, Hassan and Nilufa. **Worksheet 1.2** is an aid for pupils to learn Al-Fatihah by heart in English, but it may help them to appreciate the beauty of the original Arabic if they hear the surah recited on an audio tape or on video. The second programme in the BBC series, *Belief File: Islam*, includes a recitation of Al-Fatihah, although many can be found on the Internet. To aid concentration, you might find it helpful to ask the students to listen out for certain words, for example, *Allah*, the Arabic word for God, or *Rahim* which means Merciful, both of which can be heard twice.

Page 4

You may like to supplement your work on this section about the life of Hakeem Olajuwon. He features in a video called simply *Hakeem Olajuwon*. This includes an interview with him, and a speech by him. It is available from Sound Vision (see address list).

1.2 How do Muslims find out how Allah wants them to live?

The main aim of this investigation is for students to understand how sources of authority might be used by Muslims to make moral decisions. The point to emphasise from the opening paragraph is that it is not always easy to know what is right and good, and even if people know, it is another thing to do it! Muslims do not think they know all the answers, but they do believe Allah does.

This article by Dr Darsh is the first of many extracts from and references to *Trends* magazine. *Trends* is not the only magazine published for young Muslims – you may also like to collect copies of *Muslim News* or *Q–News* (see address list).

Back issues of *Trends* are available. In these you will find regular articles by Dr Darsh, and by other leaders or scholars of Islam. You could use them to extend activity 1 to other areas of concern for young people.

You should also draw students' attention to the point made about sources of authority at the beginning of the Student's Book, on page ii. They need to remember that people who practise a particular faith are not necessarily experts on its laws and teachings. Some Muslims, like Dr Darsh, spend their whole lifetime studying the sources of authority and become experts, but others do not. Students of religious education need to be cautious about quoting an ordinary believer as a source of authority for a particular view, unless that view is supported by a higher authority, which for Muslims would be the Qur'an or the Hadith. **Worksheet 1.3** provides help for less able students to make notes on Dr Darsh's article. This will be useful for this section and for investigation 4.2, on marriage, in Unit 4.

The diagram on page 7, and the work on it on page 8, could equally well be done using four cards (Qur'an, Sunnah, Hadith, Shari'ah), and a sheet of A3 paper on which students have to place and connect the cards appropriately.

Extension work could consider where on this sheet you might place sirah (biographical writings about Muhammad ﷺ). This caused much discussion among the authors and advisory team!

Islam in today's world Teacher's Resource Book

UNIT 1

How do sources of authority relate to each other?

The Qur'an

Pupils studying sources of authority in Islam ideally need access to the texts. The most widely accepted translation of the Qur'an is that by Abdullah Yusuf Ali. The text is printed in Arabic and English. The English is not easy but the translator keeps as close to the meaning of the Arabic as possible, and where explanation is needed, this is provided as footnotes, which are sometimes extensive. (You can see examples of his footnotes in Source A on page 24.) As Muslims regard the Qur'an as the word of Allah, copies in Arabic should be treated with respect. They should be kept clean and in a high place if possible. Some Muslim charities will donate copies of the Qur'an to schools. Teachers could try writing to some of the charities on the address list on pages 14–15.

Hadith

Collections of hadith are usually beyond the resources of a secondary school. A useful volume which students will find easy to use is a collection of hadith by Bukhari entitled *The translation of the meanings of summarized Sahih Al-Bukhari Arabic English* published by Maktaba Dar-us-Salam. Curzon Press also publishes a manual of hadith called *Gardens of the Righteous* by Muhammad Zafrulla Khan. The second volume is a selection of hadith from different sources which are sorted by topic.

If you are looking for a particular hadith or think Muhammad ﷺ might have said something about a particular subject, you could use the MSA hadith database on the Internet. (However, this method is not really suitable for GCSE students because you need to know what you are looking for. For example, a search for the word *marriage* would return several hundred results.) The address is: www.usc.edu/dept/MSA/reference/searchhadith.html

Worksheet 1.4 supports question 4 on page 8. Make sure students appreciate the important point made on page 9 about the way Muslims use sources of authority in real life. This is important because students (and teachers) often get an unrealistic and simplistic idea about the way religious believers use written sources.

In particular, it is rare that believers use isolated texts as triggers for belief or action. Where they appear to do so it is more usual that they are using this text as a symbol or starting-point for a whole train of thought or belief associated with it. This point is returned to on page 24 where we explore the range of meanings that are associated with surah 112. The key point is that believers work from principles of which the Qur'an quotes are examples. These quotes are not self-standing. So while it will be useful for students to know certain quotes for their exam, these quotes are not the only source of that belief. They are not proof texts.

The 'science' of hadith

While hadith are a lesser authority than the Qur'an, it is important for students to realise how carefully the authenticity of the hadith have been checked. There is a whole 'science' of hadith which is too complex to explore at this level; suffice to say that the provenance of the hadith – that is, who heard it, who reported it, who passed it on, and who recorded it – is a vitally important ingredient of its authority and acceptability.

Pages 10–11

The Moral Ocean

The investigation on pages 10–11 returns very deliberately to the experience of the student.
SAVE AS ... Worksheet 1.5 provides a copy of the Moral Ocean for students and a sheet to help students to record examples of people who have taken an absolute or relative stance on issues. Students will need to be reminded throughout the course to look out for such examples to record.

1.3 Islam is ...

Students have been introduced to the beliefs of Muslims and the sources of authority they might use in moral decision-making. They have discussed how these ideas might relate to their own views of the world, and the way they make decisions. In this investigation the beliefs are explored in more depth, building on the ideas about belief introduced in investigation 1.1

Page 14

Question 1 raises an important GCSE concept but also suggests a possible stereotype of Islam as an absolutist and monolithic faith. The BBC schools programme *Belief File: Islam*, is useful to reinforce the ideas from this investigation. Likewise, the CEM publication *Faith in the Future*, which is a collection of quotations from young people talking about their faith during the RE Festival in 1998, would supplement Source C on page 13.

1.4 Who are the Muslims?

It is important that students recognise that Islam is, in every sense, a world religion. They need to be encouraged to break away from the stereotype that Islam is a religion practised exclusively by people in the Indian sub-continent, or the Arabs. One of the aims of the Student's Book is to counteract this stereotype, and this investigation provides the key ideas upon which students can build a view of Islam as a world religion practised by more than a million people in Britain today, and by many different ethnic groups.

This investigation also deals with the differences between Sunni and Shi'ah. Students may well be aware of these terms. In particular the terms have been widely reported in the context of Iran and Iraq, where the two

UNIT 1

traditions have acquired a political resonance. However, the original distinctions are to do with theological authority. It is particularly important to stress that on most practical issues there is little or no divergence of opinion between Sunni and Shi'ah viewpoints, or no greater difference than between different communities of Sunnis.

1.5 How can individual Muslims change the world around them?

For some specifications, this investigation may seem out of place since 'The individual in society' figures as part of the Relationships topic (Unit 4). However, in our own planning and teaching we found that these case studies fit best here, as contrasting examples of the application of Islam in today's world. They could equally well be used as part of Unit 4.

The first case study in this investigation focuses on the Muslim Women's Helpline. Teachers can write to the Helpline for more information, enclosing a stamped addressed envelope (but please be aware that it is a charity and that materials such as back issues of *A Small Kindness* and Annual Reports need to be paid for).

Worksheet 1.6 provides a structure through which students can make notes on the history and work of the Helpline and record a personal reflection on the ideas that underlie its work.

The second case study deals with a South African Muslim called Farid Esack. Articles by him can be found on the Internet, and he has written several books. His book, called *On Being a Muslim*, published by Oneworld Press, will make interesting reading for teachers. Short excerpts, for example the section 'Where does this book come from?' on pages 3–8, may be used for more able pupils, to help them understand more about the background to this investigation.

WORKSHEET 1.1

Al-Fatihah

1. Read extract A below, from Al-Fatihah.
2. Use a coloured pen to underline the part of Al-Fatihah that Hassan, on page 2, is referring to.
3. Draw a line from it to one of the note boxes.
4. In the box, write down how he understands the words.
5. Now repeat the process for extract B.
6. **If you can**: Look at the remaining parts of Al-Fatihah (extracts C–E). Write your comments about each in the remaining boxes.

Al-Fatihah (The Opening)

A *In the name of Allah, Most Gracious, Most Merciful.*

B *Praise be to Allah,
The Cherisher and Sustainer of the Worlds;*

C *Most Gracious, Most Merciful;
Master of the Day of Judgement.*

D *It is You that we worship
And to You alone do we turn for help.*

E *Show us the straight way,
The way of those people
To whom You have shown Your Grace,
Those who have not made You Angry
And do not go astray.*

Note: It should help you in the exam if you can quote from this surah. Use Worksheet 1.2 to help you learn Al-Fatihah by heart.

WORKSHEET 1.2

How can I memorise the words of Al-Fatihah?

If you are able to memorise this key text it should help you in your exam, but more importantly it will help you to appreciate some core ideas of Muslim belief.

A

The passage on Worksheet 1.1 is divided into five parts.

1. Learn each part in turn by saying it over and over again until you can remember it. A Muslim might do this holding prayer beads.
2. Now see if you can remember two parts at a time.
3. Keep adding one more part at a time until you can manage all five.

B

If you find the exercise above difficult, you can use this memory game to learn it. You can also use this approach to learn other information for your exam.

1. Cut out the cards below and shuffle them. Place them face down on a table.
2. Remove one card without looking at it (if you cheat, you will only cheat yourself!).
3. Turn over all the remaining cards so that you can read them.
4. Which one is missing?

In the name of Allah,	Most Gracious, Most Merciful.
Praise be to Allah,	The Cherisher and Sustainer of the Worlds;
Most Gracious, Most Merciful;	Master of the Day of Judgement.
It is You that we worship	And to You alone do we turn for help.
Show us the straight way.	The way of those people
To whom You have shown Your Grace, Those who have not made You Angry	And do not go astray.

WORKSHEET 1.3 sheet 1

Dr Darsh's advice on marriage

A student has made a set of notes on Dr Darsh's teaching (see pages 6 and 7 of the Student's Book). Unfortunately they have been muddled up. You will be able to use them for your own notes if you re-arrange them under the following headings.

> Can a girl/boy choose her/his own partner?

> What should one look for in a partner?

> Can a parent refuse a proposal from a good Muslim for his daughter on the basis that the suitor is not of the same race/caste?

> Are secret marriages allowed, e.g. where girls or boys marry without parental consent, knowledge or approval?

You shouldn't get married in secret. The prophet Muhammad ﷺ said you should publicise your marriage as much as possible. Marriages should take place with a guardian and two male witnesses.

Young people who want to discuss marriage with their parents should be sensible about it and show respect for their parents.

A hadith teaches that parents should accept proposals from men who want to marry their daughters if they are good, religious men. (Does Dr Darsh mean that in some cases marriages based on falling in love might happen?)

In the past, families have arranged marriages for their children, trying to set up meetings with people they liked. In the past, if a girl did not object (was silent) she gave her approval. Girls today have more education and experience. They are not goods to be bought and sold.

A hadith says people look for beauty, nobility, wealth or religious inclination in their partners. It suggests that you will be more successful if you look for religious inclination in a person more than all the other qualities.

All people are equal. Racism is condemned in many hadith. Parents should not be allowed to refuse proposals from Muslims who come from a different ethnic group; things may change in Britain over the next few years. Meanwhile, be patient, argue your case sensitively and try not to offend your parents.

Marriage is a life-long relationship. People should look for partners who have a similar culture, family background and education. This helps the couple to understand and communicate with each other. This brings stability and success. For Muslims in a minority, the most important thing to consider is shared religion.

© John Murray — *Islam in today's world Teacher's Resource Book*

WORKSHEET 1.3 sheet 2

Once you have organised your notes, write your opinions on this sheet using complete sentences.

I particularly agree with Dr Darsh's view on marriage when he says _____

_____

_____

_____

_____

I agree with this statement because _____

_____

_____

_____

_____

_____

_____

_____

_____

_____

I do not agree with Dr Darsh when he says _____

_____

_____

_____

_____

I disagree with this statement because _____

_____

_____

_____

_____

_____

_____

_____

_____

_____

WORKSHEET 1.4

How might a Muslim follow the example of Muhammad ﷺ?

You can use this worksheet for question 4 on page 8.
Muslims don't only learn from what Muhammad ﷺ *said*. They also learn from what he *did*. They see his actions as a model. Some attempt to copy him literally – 'Muhammad ﷺ did it this way, so I will.' Others try to find the principle in his action and apply it to their own lives.

Listed in the table below, in the first column, are seven exemplary actions that Muhammad ﷺ did.

1 In the second column write the principle which lies behind each action.
2 In the third column write how a person today might copy or adapt that action. You might think they can and should copy Muhammad ﷺ literally. You might think they can adapt it so that they still follow the principle of Muhammad's ﷺ action.
3 As you read this book, record three more actions of Muhammad ﷺ in the blank rows, and show the principle and application for those actions.

Muhammad ﷺ	Principle	Application
1 … made his welfare payments in barley.	Be generous to the poor. Give the poor what is most useful to them.	Give payments in money or food.
2 … performed the five prayers at the set time.		
3 … cut off a corner of his cloak rather than disturbing the cat and her kittens who had fallen asleep on it.		
4 … built a mosque as a meeting place for others on his own premises.		
5 … when a woman who had insulted him fell ill, he did all her housework until she got better.		
6 … worked hard and was always totally fair in his business dealings.		
7 … refused great riches and lived a simple life, often living off dates, barley and water.		
8 …		
9 …		
10 …		

© John Murray   *Islam in today's world Teacher's Resource Book*

WORKSHEET 1.5 sheet 1

The Muslim Moral Ocean

Making moral decisions is a bit like steering a ship through dangerous or exciting unknown waters. To help you reach a decision you are happy about and which you feel is right, there are 'islands' you can visit. These islands are your 'sources of moral authority'.

Islands shown: Conscience, Secular wisdom, Shari'ahs, Writings of Muslim scholars, 5 pillars of faith, DECISION I SHOULD MAKE, Hadith, Sunnah, Muslim leaders, Qur'an, Friends, Dad, Mum, Wider family, Christianity, Muslim magazines and newspapers, Teenage magazines, Judaism.

WHAT SHALL I DO?

1 Plot the route you think a Muslim would take across the Moral Ocean. They can call at five islands before making their decision. Make sure they visit their most important island first.
2 What differences, if any, are there between a Muslim's route and the route you might take? You may want to label the empty islands.

WORKSHEET 1.5 sheet 2

Absolute and relative morality

ABSOLUTE MORALITY – this is when a person believes that there is a right course of action in a moral dilemma that is true in all situations, regardless of culture, religious tradition, time or age. For example: 'it is always wrong to kill'.

RELATIVE MORALITY – this is when a person has strong beliefs or principles but they believe that different courses of action might be needed in different situations. For example: 'it is usually wrong to kill, but sometimes it might be necessary for a particular reason'.

Use this worksheet for the **SAVE AS...** task on page 10.

In your exam you may need to give examples of people who have absolute or relative views on various moral issues. You may also need to refer to religious traditions (e.g. Qur'an and Hadith) and to groups that demonstrate these views. As you work through the course, note down on this sheet examples of each. Make sure that you note clearly where you found these examples so that you can refer back to them.

One example from your book is given to start you off. But don't limit yourself to what is in the book. Include examples you have read elsewhere or seen on television. You will probably need to continue on a separate sheet.

You will not be able to get an example of both absolute and relative morality for every issue. You will also find that you have many more entries in one column than the other. You will be able to discuss in class why that is.

Issue	An absolutist example (include reference to source)	A relativist example (include reference to source)
Abortion	A. Majid Katme believes that abortion at any time is wrong because '...the soul is breathed in by the first 42 days of pregnancy.' (Source B on page 54 of Student's Book)	N. Mahjoub says, 'Some [Muslim] jurists permit [abortion] before the 120 days under certain conditions (the poor health of the mother, in the case of rape, etc.).' (Source C on page 54 of Student's Book)

WORKSHEET 1.6

Information file: The Muslim Women's Helpline

Use the information on pages 18 and 19 of the Student's Book to answer the following questions. Include your own response at the end.

1. When did the Helpline begin? _____

2. Why did the women start the Helpline? (Don't forget to include the distinctively Muslim reasons.)
   _____
   _____

3. Give examples of three things that the Helpline does.
   _____
   _____
   _____

4. Explain how the Helpline supported one particular woman.
   _____
   _____
   _____

5. Why is the Helpline newsletter called *A Small Kindness*?
   _____
   _____
   _____

6. Are men involved in the Helpline's work? Give evidence to support your answer.
   _____

On reflection ...

7. Complete the following sentences to sum up your views on the Helpline's work.

- I think that the work of the Muslim Women's Helpline is _____
  _____

  I think this because _____
  _____

- One thing that really impressed me was _____
  _____
  _____

- If I had a chance to try and change the world I would like to _____
  _____
  _____

- I think this would be really important because _____
  _____
  _____

WORKSHEET 1.7

Examination practice: The individual in society

As you answer this question, use only information on Islam.

a) Outline and explain the teachings about service to others in one religious tradition. (9)

b) How does one religious tradition put its teachings into practice in the community? (6)

c) 'People who spend their time doing things for others without deepening their spiritual lives will have nothing of real value to give to others.'
Do you agree? Give reasons for your answer, showing that you have thought about more than one point of view. (5)

NEAB, 1998

WORKSHEET 1.8

End of Unit Quiz: An Islamic world view

Test yourself or your neighbour with this quick quiz.

1. What is the Qur'an?
2. What is the Arabic name of the first surah of the Qur'an? What does it mean in English?
3. State two beliefs expressed in the first surah of the Qur'an.
4. If a Muslim does more good than bad in their life, how will they be rewarded?
5. What do Muslims mean by the phrase *the straight way*?
6. What is the Sunnah?
7. What are hadith?
8. Give one example of a hadith.
9. What does the phrase *absolute morality* mean?
10. What does the phrase *relative morality* mean?
11. What does *iman* mean?
12. How many key beliefs does Islam have?
13. How many pillars of faith does Islam have?
14. What does the Shahadah state?
15. When might a Muslim say it?
16. What is sawm?
17. Give one example of a haram action.
18. Give one example of a halal action.
19. What is the mission statement of the Muslim Women's Helpline?
20. Why is Farid Esack controversial?

UNIT 2
Thinking about Allah

Overview: Islamic theology

The aim of the unit is to give students a clear understanding of the distinctive nature of Islamic theology. The first investigation (2.1) explores the nature of Allah; the second (2.2) the nature of revelation; the third (2.3) the Muslim explanations of and response to evil and suffering. Philosophical arguments about the existence of God are not dealt with in this volume, but in *Christianity in today's world* in the context of Christian examples, since the syllabuses do not require investigating these in more than one tradition.

Note: The title of this unit is 'Thinking about Allah'. The Arabic word *Allah*, meaning 'God' has been used throughout, and pupils should be encouraged to use it when referring to Muslim beliefs about God. We have also tried not to use the anthropomorphic pronoun *He* of Allah, although most of the sources do.

Starting strategies

Most teachers find teaching theology a challenge, especially when students in their class may range from those who firmly do not believe in God in any form, to those who do – with every shade of disagreement in between. Religious Education teachers are told to begin their exploration of a new topic at their students' level of understanding, but in this area many are at no point at all!

When teaching about Allah, it is often refreshing to begin – as this unit does – with the simplicity of the Shahadah. Islam begins with the assumption that everyone is born a Muslim, that somewhere inside every human being is a need to worship their Creator. The Muslim declaration of faith is not a complex set of theological principles, but two simple statements. Students need to know that if they can understand these statements, they have the foundations on which the rest of Islamic theology can be built.

Other resources

Programme 1 from the BBC Schools series *Belief File: Islam*, which is called 'The Shahadah', could provide a useful introduction to this unit. It presents the beliefs in a clear and straightforward way, and is accessible to students of a wide range of abilities.

2.1 The One and Only ...

The opening paragraph of this investigation makes the simple but important point that Allah is, by definition, beyond our understanding. So the issue for a Muslim is not, 'How can I understand something that is beyond my understanding?' but 'If Allah is so great, beyond my understanding, then I must worship Him.'

Students could begin by completing **Worksheets 2.1** and **2.2**, which help them to understand the surah and Yusuf Ali's points. We wanted the notes to keep some of Yusuf Ali's distinctive (and difficult) style, but Worksheet 2.1 further simplifies the language of the notes for those who need help.

You may then like to use Source A as the basis for discussing students' own viewpoints and beliefs. Groups of two or three could each take one belief and decide if they agree or disagree with it, explaining why others may disagree with them.

Page 25
How does belief in Tawhid affect a Muslim's life?

Some teachers prefer to introduce the idea of Tawhid within the context of monotheism and polytheism in Arabia at the time of Muhammad ﷺ. As the Checkpoint on page 25 makes clear, 'Tawhid' was *the* big message. Students will enjoy excerpts from the feature film, *The Message*. It is a well-produced film, available on video (see address list), with many well-known actors in the leading roles. Muhammad ﷺ, of course, is not shown. Many scenes are seen as if through his eyes, and the result is quite satisfactory once you are used to this device. After the first few minutes of the film, the story goes back to the year when Muhammad ﷺ received the first revelation from Allah, and students will be able to appreciate what Makkah might have been like at that time.

A different approach would be to start with the 'If there is One God ...'-list at the top of page 25, and see if pupils can extend it.

Worksheet 2.3 supports question 2 on page 25 by making links between Tawhid and certain positive personal qualities.

Pages 26–7
The 'names' of Allah

Muslims do not draw pictures to represent Allah. They believe that Allah is beyond our comprehension and therefore cannot be represented. Page 26 features a stunning work of Islamic art, *The Attributes of Divine Perfection* by Ahmed Moustafa. Other examples of Islamic calligraphic art, a diverse and wonderful art form, can be found elsewhere in the book. Many art galleries around the country have collections of Islamic traditional and contemporary art, including the use of calligraphy and geometric patterns. An exciting way of exploring Muslim ideas about Allah would be to visit one such gallery, such as the Zamana Gallery in London or St Mungo's in

UNIT 2

Glasgow, to discover how creating a piece of art can be an act of worship.

There are several different translations of the 99 names of Allah. A full list is found as **Worksheet 2.4** which supports Activity 1 on page 27.

Worksheet 2.5 provides an opportunity for students to explore this art form for themselves.

Page 28
Immanent and transcendent

Examination specifications do not require these terms to be studied in great depth at this level. However, these ideas are important for all Muslims as they try to develop their relationship with Allah, and some students become fascinated by the apparent contradiction between the two terms, which justifies spending a little more time.

For the Sufis these ideas take on a great significance. Sufism is explored on page 38.

Worksheet 2.6 could be used as part of this investigation, or at the end to assess how the ideas have been understood. This sheet will involve students using their knowledge and understanding of immanence and transcendence and reflecting on their study of this topic.

2.2 How is Allah revealed to human beings?

This investigation comprises eleven pages exploring different aspects of revelation.

- **Page 29** introduces key ideas about revelation which students will need to be aware of for their examination.
- **Pages 30–1** explore the way that, for Muslims, creation is a means of general revelation.
- **Pages 34–8** investigate religious experience.
- Finally, **page 39** offers a review task to pull it all together.

Page 29
Fitrah is an intrinsically interesting idea and could provoke a worthwhile discussion. It is also in marked contrast to the view of 'original sin' which some students may hold. What evidence is there for each belief?

Pages 32–3
This important spread begins with FAQs (frequently asked questions) and then focuses on Allah's final revelation, the Qur'an, which was revealed through the 'seal of the prophets', Muhammad ﷺ.

In Source E, the illustration of the 25 prophets mentioned in the Qur'an, you will see many familiar names from Judaism and Christianity. Teachers may like to use the story of Jonah, from the Independent Television series *Testament* as an illustration of how prophets were sent to specific nations at a particular time in their history and all brought the same message. The *Belief File: Islam* programme, 'The Qur'an', describes the unique nature of this revelation: it is the final revelation for all people, for all time.

Page 34
In this case study we investigate how these forms of revelation can lead people to Allah.

Most students will not have heard of Cat Stevens, although some teachers may have his albums. Contemporary and popular music does often ask the ultimate questions which are the essence of Religious Education. You will find plenty of examples of this sort in Cat Stevens' lyrics. On his home page on the Internet, you can listen to some of his old music and the new material he has recorded as Yusuf Islam. This is unaccompanied except for the drum, according to Islamic tradition. You can also download a video clip about the making of the video, 'The Life of the Last Prophet'.

The Internet address is: www.catstevens.com. This site has many links to information about his current work within the Muslim community, and interviews past and present. The full lyrics for 'I wish I wish' can be found on this site at www.catstevens.com/media/

Page 35
The **FOCUS TASK** is supported by **Worksheet 2.8**.
ICT ACTIVITY There have been many references in these notes to the use of the Internet for exploring Islam. One word of warning: surfing the Internet is the easiest way to waste time. It is very easy to get side-tracked. On a practical note: if you have a choice of when to use the Internet, you should use it earlier in the day, because the information will tend to download more quickly at that time.

Worksheet 2.9 allows those with access to the Internet to explore some stories of converts or reverts to Islam. If your ICT resources are minimal, it is still worthwhile, as a teacher, investigating the materials, and printing some of them out for class use.

Pages 36–7
These pages focus on salah. Students will not be required to know each specific movement in the prayer for the examination, but they should understand the part that salah plays in worship and how it helps Muslims to become closer to Allah by obediently submitting to Allah's will. **Worksheet 2.10** supports this aim, and **2.11** supports the **SAVE AS ...** task on page 37.

Page 39
DISCUSSION The Hodja/Nazruddin stories proliferate in the Muslim press and can be found on the Internet at http://turkey.org./groupd/chapter1/nhodja2.htm. This discussion activity might seem a trivial aside on a big issue, but here again our strategy has been to offer an in-depth exploration of this philosophical issue of real or illusory experience within another book in the series, *Christianity in today's world* (pages 98–9).

The **FOCUS TASK** on page 39 draws the ideas of the last ten pages together. **Worksheet 2.11** saves students writing it all out again themselves.

Students could learn more about Sufism on the Internet site of the Naqshbandi Sufi order: naqshbandi.net. To read some beautiful sufi poetry which further explores the idea of immanence in Islam, try the following address: www.naqshbandi.net/haqqani/sufi/saints/Rumi_poetry.html

2.3 Why is suffering part of Allah's plan?

Every RE teacher knows that if you go to a party and admit what you do for a living, you will sooner or later get the question, 'OK, so if there's a God, how come he allows people to suffer?' Most of us somehow manage to dodge the question, but our short course students cannot.

In some specifications, this theme is part of the work on the existence of God (we have covered the rest of it in *Christianity in today's world*). However:

- the issue of suffering is central to most specifications and to students' own questions about religion
- Muslim ideas about suffering are distinctive and interesting
- suffering is essential background to work on Unit 3 issues of life and death, and so we have gone into it in some depth.

In dealing with this investigation, teachers will need to be sensitive to the fact that students may have a recent or current experience of suffering. Some students may wish to talk about their experiences, and teachers may need to remind students of the need to be sensitive to the feelings of their classmates.

Page 40

The illustration on this page tries in a light-hearted and hopefully inoffensive way to introduce this issue, and also cover the distinction between suffering caused by humans, and natural suffering, which is essential for any response to the question of suffering.

Worksheet 2.12 supports Activity 4 on page 40 which allows students to ensure that they understand this distinction.

The remainder of this investigation is structured around four big ideas in Muslim responses to suffering. These are summarised in the Focus Task on page 41.

Page 42

Allah has a plan. The Muslim belief of Qadr can loosely be translated as predestination, but, as the graphic makes clear, it means more than that.

Page 43

Humans have free will. Worksheet 2.13 tells the story of creation from surah 2 of the Qur'an, which is required knowledge on some syllabuses and supports the Activity on page 43.

ACTIVITY You will need to refer students back to the Checkpoint on page 41.

Page 44

Suffering is a test for the next life. It is essential that students understand that, for Muslims, this life is not the only life. It will be impossible for them to make sense of many other investigations unless they grasp this basic fact, even if they do not share this belief in life after death, and judgement.

Page 45

Good can come from suffering. Source F is an eloquent personal investigation of Sarah Joseph's experience of suffering. However, it is also full of potential for discussion about Muslim ideas on life after death. She uses some complex phrases – 'We are all dying', 'Death – the only absolute in our lives' – which could be discussed.

This 'theological' and reflective source could stand usefully alongside the more descriptive and pragmatic approach to death of Moona Taslim-Saif on pages 50–51.

Worksheet 2.13 explores a wider set of experiences and provides an opportunity to assess students' understanding of the Muslim teachings they have studied.

Page 46

This Review Task would ideally be set up as a class debate with speakers on both sides. For an example of how to do this, you could watch the BBC in-service training programme on Religious Education, *Four Lessons and a Funeral*, which includes a short section on a Key Stage 4 class who role play a debate.

If you can arrange to video the experience, or have the students video it, this would be even better, because it gives you the opportunity to evaluate the success of the exercise later, and to show future classes highlights so that they understand how it might be done.

Worksheet 2.15 is a writing frame which may be used for the written task of replying in role as a Muslim.

Worksheets 2.16, **2.17** and **2.18** are an examination question, quotation cards and end of unit quiz to help pupils prepare for the written examination paper.

WORKSHEET 2.1

He is Allah

1 Read carefully the notes around the surah below. On this worksheet the notes have been simplified.
  Note 1 applies to the entire surah. The other notes refer to a specific place in the surah. Try to connect each of notes 2–8 with one word or line from the surah.
2 Give each note a heading. Use your own words.

1 Here we are taught to avoid the mistakes people fall into in trying to understand Allah.

2 His nature is far beyond our limited minds, so we try to feel He is a Person.

3 All beings are made by Him. They cannot be compared with Him.

4 This verse rejects polytheism, a belief in many gods.

Say:
He is Allah,
The One and Only;
Allah, the Eternal, Absolute;
He begot none,
Nor was He begotten;
And there is none like Him.

5 He is without beginning or end.

6 He is not limited by time or place.

7 This is to reject the Christian idea of the Trinity: God as 'Father', Jesus as 'Son', etc.

8 This sums up the whole argument and warns us not to think of Allah in human terms.

Surah 112.1–4, called Al-Ikhlas (Purity of Faith), with notes adapted from notes by Abdullah Yusuf Ali

WORKSHEET 2.2

About Allah

On this chart you are going to record ideas about Allah.

1. Start with what you found in Surah Al-Ikhlas 112.1–4 on page 24. Write your key words on the 'legs' of the spider diagram.
2. Add to it as you study pages 26–7.
3. Add to it again at the end of each unit of this course.

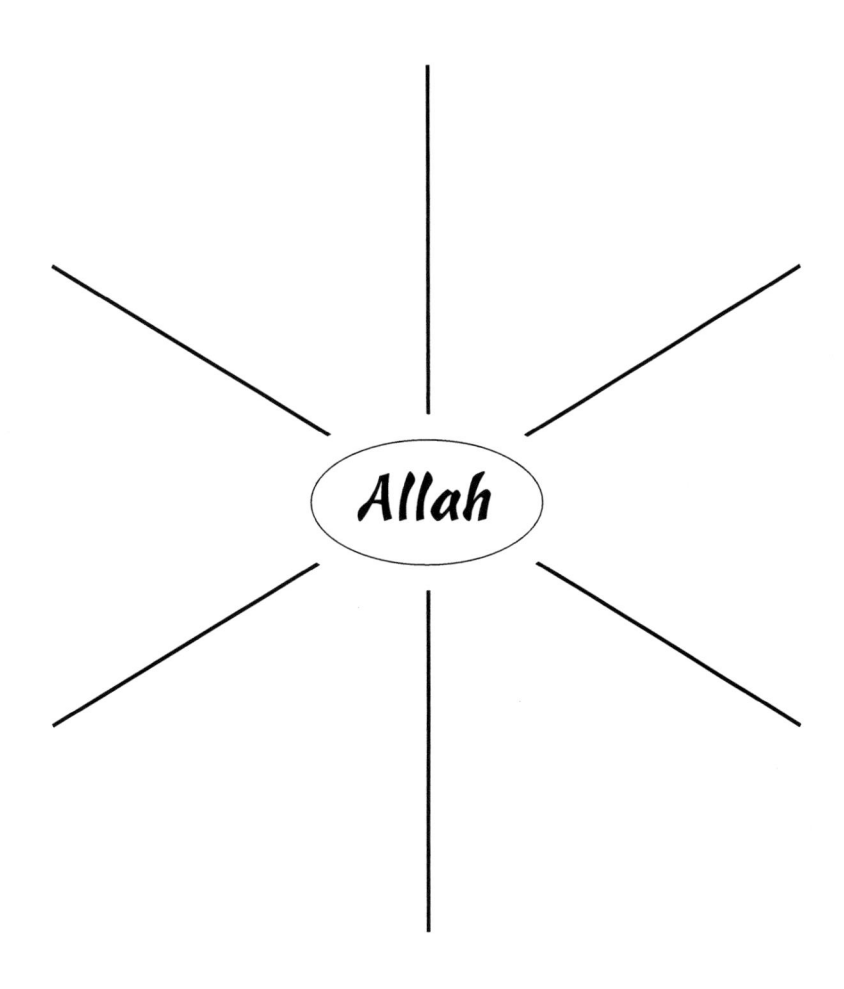

WORKSHEET 2.3

What does it mean to believe in Tawhid?

How might the personal qualities below come from a belief in Tawhid?
Read the statements on the right and try to match each to a personal quality.

Qualities

- Obedience
- Determination
- Contentment
- Bravery
- Honesty
- Modesty
- Self-respect
- Respect for the environment

Statements

- I realise that I am nothing without Allah who created me.
- I realise that Allah knows everything I do; I cannot hide from him.
- I realise that the mercy and compassion of Allah, the One and Only, include me.
- I want to help take care of Allah's wonderful creation.
- I will live and die a Muslim; my faith is my life.
- I trust in Allah: my faith brings me great strength.
- I want to follow the path that leads me to truth.
- I realise that the true way is the best way for my life.
- I am a better person as a Muslim than I was before I changed my life.
- I realise that Allah has given me the perfect guide in the Qur'an and the life of His final prophet, Muhammad ﷺ.
- I feel closer to Allah.

Complete the following sentence as many times as you wish.

- I think a belief in Tawhid might help a person to _____

because _____

_____

Islam in today's world Teacher's Resource Book   © John Murray

WORKSHEET 2.4

The 99 names of Allah

Here is a list of the 99 names of Allah, with their English translations. Try to group the names by colour-coding them as follows.

Names relating to Allah's role as:

- judge
- creator
- controller of human life
- beyond human understanding
- carer
- other.

Allah	God	Ash Shahid	The Witness
Al-Rahman	The Compassionate	Al-Haqq	The Truth
Al-Rahim	The Merciful	Al-Wakil	The Trustee
Al-Malik	The King	Al-Qawi	The Strong
Al-Quddus	The Holy	Al-Matin	The Firm
As-Salam	The Peace	Al-Wali	The Friend
Al-Mu'min	The One with Faith	Al-Hamid	The Praiseworthy
Al-Muhaymin	The Protector	Al-Muhsi	The Counter
Al-'Aziz	The Mighty	Al-Mubdi'	The Originator
Al-Jabbar	The Repairer	Al-Mu'id	The Restorer
Al-Mutakabbir	The Imperious	Al-Muhyi	The Life-Giver
Al-Khaliq	The Creator	Al-Mumit	The Death-Giver
Al-Bari'	The Maker	Al-Hayy	The Living
Al-Musawwir	The Fashioner	Al-Qayyum	The Self-Subsistent
Al-Ghaffar	The Forgiver	Al-Wajid	The Finder
Al-Qahhar	The Dominant	Al-Majid	The Noble
Al-Wahhab	The Bestower	Al-Ahad	The One
Al-Razzaq	The Provider	As-Samad	The Eternal
Al-Fattah	The Opener	Al-Qadir	The Able
Al-'Alim	The Knower	Al-Muqtadir	The Powerful
Al-Qaibid	The Contractor	Al-Muqaddim	The Expediter
Al-Basit	The Expander	Al-Mu'akhkhir	The Deferrer
Al-Khafid	The Humbler	Al-Awwal	The First
Al-Rafi'	The Exalter	Al-Akhir	The Last
Al-Mu'izz	The Honorer	Az-Zahir	The Manifest
Al-Mudhill	The Abaser	Al-Batin	The Hidden
As Sami'	The Hearer	Al-Wali	The Governor
Al-Basir	The Seer	Al-Muta'ali	The Exalted
Al-Hakam	The Judge	Al-Barr	The Benefactor
Al-'Adl	The Just	At-Tawwab	The Acceptor of Repentance
Al-Latif	The Subtle	Al-Muntaqim	The Avenger
Al-Khabir	The Aware	Al-'Afuw	The Pardoner
Al-Halim	The Gentle	Ar Ra'uf	The Pardoner
Al-'Azim	The Mighty	Malik al-Mulk	The Ruler of the Kingdom
Al-Ghafur	The Forgiving	Dhu 'l-Jalal wa 'l-Ikram	Lord of Majesty and Generosity
Ash Shakur	The Grateful	Al-Muqsit	The Equitable
Al-'Ali	The Lofty	Al-Jami'	The Gatherer
Al-Kabir	The Great	Al-Ghani	The Self-Sufficient
Al-Hafiz	The Guardian	Al-Mughni	The Enricher
Al-Muqit	The Nourisher	Al-Mani	The Preventer
Al-Hasib	The Reckoner	Ad-Darr	The Distresser
Al-Jalil	The Majestic	An-Nafi'	The Benefactor
Al-Karim	The Generous	An-Nur	The Light
Ar Raqib	The Watcher	Al-Hadi	The Guide
Al-Mujib	The Responder	Al-Badi	The Incomparable
Al-Wasi'	The Englober	Al-Baqi	The Enduring
Al-Hakim	The Wise	Al-Warith	The Inheritor
Al-Wadud	The Loving	Ar Rashid	The Rightly Guided
Al-Majid	The Glorious	As Sabur	The Patient
Al-Ba'ith	The Resurrector		

WORKSHEET 2.5

Calligraphy, shape and pattern

A Muslim artist might try to praise Allah through a non-figurative piece of art (that is, not using any figures or bodies). Instead, they might use calligraphy, shape and pattern.

1. Re-read surah 112.1–4 (you will find it on page 24), and pick out the key words that describe the nature of Allah. Write them in the box on the right.
2. Try to decide what shapes on this pattern and what colours best represent these descriptions.
3. Colour in this sheet, trying to communicate your understanding of surah 112 in what you produce.
4. Now complete a second sheet, this time identifying your own or different beliefs and ideas about Allah in the shapes and colours.

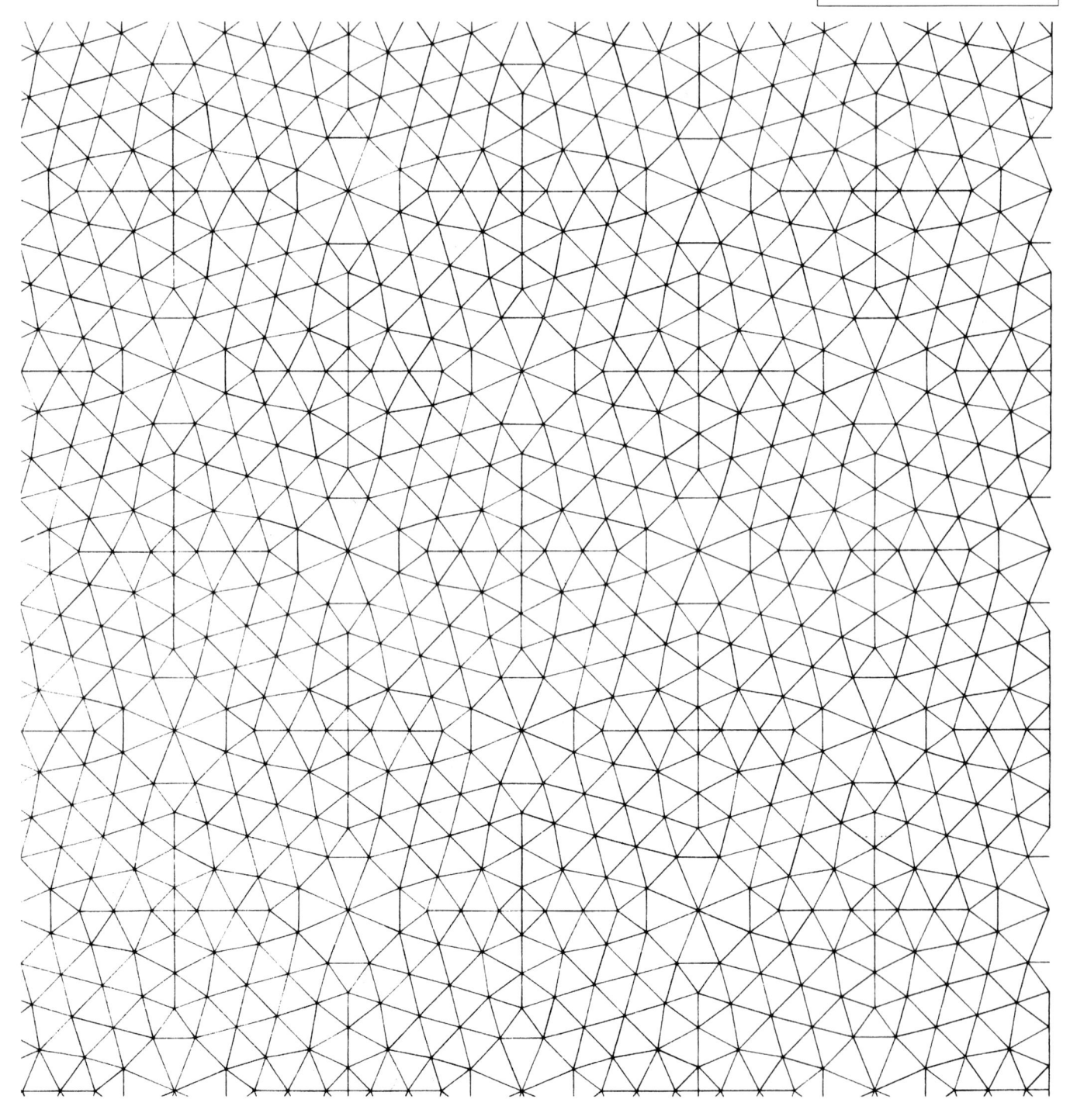

WORKSHEET 2.6

Immanent and transcendent

1. Read the following statements about Allah and decide whether they express a belief in
   a) Allah's transcendence *or*
   b) Allah's immanence *or*
   c) neither.

   1. I feel the presence of Allah close to me as I live my life.
   2. He is Allah, the One and Only.
   3. Who is it that rules and regulates all affairs?
   4. Allah the Eternal, the Absolute …
   5. No Muslim should ever attempt to draw an image of Allah or make a statue to worship. Allah is beyond comparison with all other living things.
   6. Who is it that sustains you in life from the sky and from the Earth?
   7. Allah is closer to me than my jugular vein.

2. Using any of these examples, or your own examples if you prefer, explain how Muslim belief emphasises both the immanence and transcendence of Allah.

   This is a sample answer, with one in every six words removed. The missing words are in the box below.

   Muslims believe that Allah is _____ immanent and transcendent.

   Allah is _____ the limits of this world _____ the rules of nature or _____. For example, the Qur'an states _____ surah 112, 'He is Allah, _____ One and Only; Allah, the _____, Absolute;' This passage explains how _____ was neither born nor is _____ father to any other creation. _____ is beyond comparison with any _____ living thing.

   At the same _____, Muslims believe Allah is immanent, _____ is to say close to _____ life and acting in human _____. The Qur'an also states 'Allah _____ closer to you than your jugular vein.' (_____ 50.16) Allah knows everything that is _____ and said. Nothing is hidden _____ him.

surah	done	the	that	Eternal	outside	including	time	in
Allah	from	affairs	Allah	other	human	is	time	both	He

On reflection…

3. Complete the following sentences to sum up your views on these ideas.

   - I find the belief that Allah is **transcendent** convincing/unconvincing because I think

   _____
   _____

   - I find the belief that Allah is **immanent** convincing/unconvincing because I think

   _____
   _____

   - One thing I have learned from these ideas is _____

   _____
   _____

WORKSHEET 2.7 sheet 1

Makkah: 610CE

This is RE, not history or geography! However, Islam has its roots in a particular place and a particular time. To understand Islam it will help if you understand some of its history and some of its geography. So here goes: our snappy summary of the origins of Islam. On the next page is a role play which builds on this information.

1 Muhammad ﷺ was born in Makkah in 570CE

He was orphaned at the age of six and brought up by his uncle. He was a member of the Quraysh tribe who ruled Makkah. He married a successful trades-woman called Khadijah. They lived comfortably, although they were never wealthy. Muhammad ﷺ had a good reputation in Makkah. He was known as Al-Amin (the trustworthy one).

2 Makkah was a centre for idol-worship

In the centre of Makkah was the Ka'bah. It had originally been built by the Prophet Ibrahim and his son Isma'il for the worship of Allah. Tradition says that, before that, Adam had built a place for worship on or near the site. So there was a long history of monotheism in this area.

However, by the time of Muhammad ﷺ Makkah had become a major centre of polytheistic worship. People flocked from miles around to worship the hundreds of idols and images that were kept in and around the Ka'bah. They believed the gods had power to affect people's lives. People would consult them about all sorts of things such as arranging a marriage, settling arguments and deciding the safest route for a journey.

There were people living in Arabia who believed in one God: Christians and Jews for example, and also people called Hanif who tended to live apart from the rest of society. However, these were a small minority in Makkah. The majority were polytheists.

3 Makkah was a trade centre

Makkah was at the junction of several trade routes. Many people came to the trade fairs which brought wealth to the businesses of the city. The trade fairs were particularly dependent on pilgrims coming to worship at the Ka'bah.

4 There was inequality and tension in Makkah

People lived in tribes. A tribe was a group of people with a common ancestor. The tribe who ruled Makkah was called the Quraysh. Tribes were divided into clans. Some were very powerful and rich whilst others were much weaker and poorer. There was fierce competition between the clans, and disagreement about how life in Makkah should be organised. Women's status was low, and slavery was commonplace. People who did not belong to a clan had no rights at all.

5 Muhammad ﷺ received a revelation

Muhammad ﷺ spent long periods away from Makkah, in a cave on Mount Hira, thinking deeply about idol-worship and injustice in Makkah. He often spent the whole month of Ramadan in the hills.

In the year 610CE Muhammad ﷺ was about 40 years old. In his cave he heard a voice speaking to him, commanding him to 'Recite'. Then he saw the angel Jibril who had brought him a message from Allah which he learned by heart.

6 The message said 'There is one God ...'

The message was simple: there is one God who created human beings. Later Muhammad ﷺ received another message: he was to tell the people of Makkah about the one God who would judge them after their death.

During the next 23 years, Muhammad ﷺ received many more revelations, until finally Allah had revealed the complete Qur'an.

The basic message of the Qur'an was not new. It repeated the message Allah had sent many times before, to other people. These included the prophets of the Jewish and Christian religions, from Abraham through to Jesus. Each nation had been sent a prophet, but the prophets had been rejected or their message distorted.

The Qur'an, though, was unique, because this time Allah had sent a final message through the last prophet, Muhammad ﷺ. This message was the unaltered words of Allah Himself. It was designed for all people for all time. In the final words of Allah's revelation, Allah says, 'Today I have perfected your religion for you, completed my favour upon you and have chosen Islam as your way of life.' (surah 5.3–4).

WORKSHEET 2.7 sheet 2

Makkah: 610CE

Role play

It is 610CE. Imagine your class are inhabitants of Makkah. Muhammad ﷺ has got the whole town talking because he claims to be a messenger of the One True God – Allah. He says that life and worship in Makkah must change. You must consider the case for and against Islam.

1. Divide the class into two groups. One will argue the case for Islam. The other will argue the case against it.
2. To prepare for the debate, members of each group must prepare speeches. Speakers may include:
   a) an elderly and wealthy merchant of Makkah
   b) a pilgrim visiting the idols in the Ka'bah
   c) a slave
   d) a person who recently heard Muhammad ﷺ speak about his revelations
   e) a Christian visitor to Makkah who welcomes Muhammad's ﷺ teaching about one God
   f) ordinary citizens with a range of views.
   The panels below will give you some arguments to use in your speeches but you will be able to think of others.

The case for Islam

- The central focus of life in Makkah is the Ka'bah, which was originally built as a place for monotheistic worship.

- The gods, which were made only by human hands, are false. Allah is the one true God, who made the universe and everything in it.

- People are accountable for their actions; people cannot behave just as they like without any regard for the consequences.

- Society in Makkah is unjust; most of the wealthy people do nothing to help those less fortunate than themselves, and that needs to change.

The case against Islam

- Many gods have been worshipped in Makkah for generations. Why should we change?

- Polytheism has made Makkah wealthy. Without the gods in the Ka'bah, people would stop coming for their annual pilgrimage. Without the pilgrimage, the trade fairs would not make any profit.

- If people start disagreeing about religion, there would be more disputes between families and clans.

- Poverty and inequality are part of life. People who are poor have offended the gods. Wealth and poverty, fortune and misfortune, health and sickness, are just some of the ways in which the gods show who has pleased them and who has not. We should not interfere.

- We cannot survive with only one god. The gods all have different parts to play in our lives.

WORKSHEET 2.8

Life-changing experiences

The two articles below will help you answer the Focus Task on page 35 but, as you know, you shouldn't believe everything you read in the papers! Both articles contain mistakes, so you will need to check in the Student's Book before you can use them.

Sixties star Pat Stevens (hits including 'Morning has Broken' – if you don't go back that far, this classic hymn was once trendy and in the charts) has stunned the rock and pop world by announcing his conversion to Hinduism.

Pat was staying with his girlfriend at the exclusive Palm Beach Hotel. Pat claims that while he was in the pool he nearly drowned but that God saved him. Pat allegedly called out, 'God, just save my life and I will do whatever you say!'

Maybe the wild life has finally got to Pat or he had too much of the sun that afternoon. Either way, we won't be hearing any new songs from Pat, who has announced he is quitting his musical career to concentrate on prayer and meditation.

Music Now!, August 1977

The famous singer, Wat Stevens, has reverted to Islam after a dramatic, near-death experience in California last week.

Wat was staying at his sister's house in the mountains. He was swimming in a nearby lake when he got into difficulties. Mat felt himself being dragged under the water. He though he was going to suffocate. He called out to Allah, 'Oh God, if you save me, I promise I will be good from now on.'

Suddenly he found the water pushing him back to the shore. His prayer had been answered. Allah has once again revealed his great mercy and compassion.

Muslim Herald, August 1977

WORKSHEET 2.9

My story!

The Internet carries many stories of people who have become Muslims. You can find out the reasons for and the results of their reversion.

Your teacher will have told you how to enter a WWW (World Wide Web), address into your Internet browser.

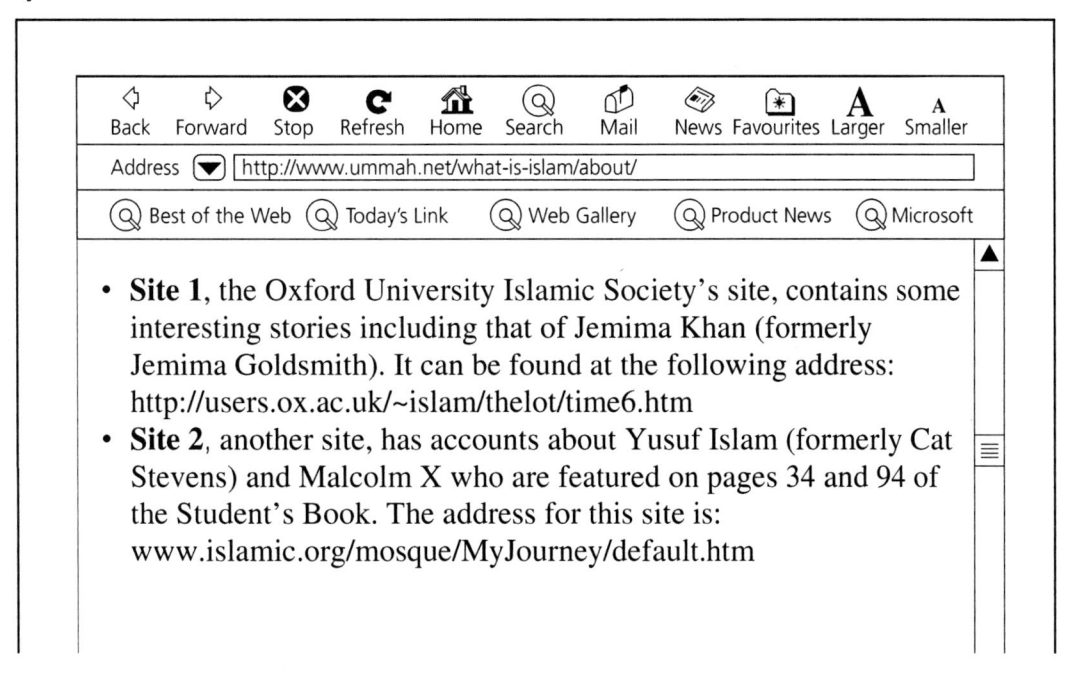

```
Address: http://www.ummah.net/what-is-islam/about/
```

- **Site 1**, the Oxford University Islamic Society's site, contains some interesting stories including that of Jemima Khan (formerly Jemima Goldsmith). It can be found at the following address: http://users.ox.ac.uk/~islam/thelot/time6.htm
- **Site 2**, another site, has accounts about Yusuf Islam (formerly Cat Stevens) and Malcolm X who are featured on pages 34 and 94 of the Student's Book. The address for this site is: www.islamic.org/mosque/MyJourney/default.htm

Choose one of the convert stories on these sites or another one you find to read, or print it out to read later. Make notes about the person's experiences, as follows:

- Did they decide to become Muslim over a long period of time, or quickly?

_____
_____
_____

- What attracted them to Islam?

_____
_____
_____

- What effect has their conversion had on their lives?

_____
_____
_____

- How did others react to their decision?

_____
_____
_____

© John Murray   *Islam in today's world Teacher's Resource Book*

WORKSHEET 2.10

Salah

Each time a Muslim performs salah they follow a set order of words and actions known as a rakah. The words and pictures below have become muddled up.

1. In order to make accurate notes in your book you will need to cut them out and re-arrange them. Try to do this without looking at the book first to see how much you can remember.
2. When you have finished, in a different colour write beside each picture a quality that the action might encourage in Muslims.
   Some suggestions are included in the box.

> Self-discipline   Obedience   A sense of peace   Community spirit
> Thankfulness   Humility

They rinse their mouth three times.

SALAH
I bear witness that there is no god but Allah and that Muhammad is the Messenger of Allah.

Facing qibla, each Muslim says how many units of salah (prayer) they intend saying.

Allah hears those who praise him. Our Lord, All Praise be to you.

Allahu Akbar. (Allah is the Greatest.)

Allah is the Greatest.

They wash their face three times, from right to left and from forehead to throat.

They pass wet hands backwards from the forehead to the neck.

They clean the back of their neck.

They clean their ears and behind their ears.

They wash their feet.

They wash both hands, up to the wrist.

They bow down twice repeating:
Allah is the Greatest. (Silent:) Glory be to my Lord, the Most High.

(Silent:) I bear witness that there is no god but Allah. I bear witness that Muhammad is His Servant and Messenger.

Finally they pray for the Prophet and for peace.

Allah is the Greatest. (Silent:) Glory be to my Great Lord and Praise be to Him.

They wash their nostrils and the tip of their nose three times.

Allah is the Greatest. (Silent:) My Lord, forgive me.

WUDU   Muslims say:

In the name of Allah, the Most Merciful, the Most Kind.

They wash each arm three times.

(Silent:) Glory and Praise be to You. Blessed is Your Name and Exalted is Your Majesty.

They bow down twice repeating:
Allah is the Greatest. (Silent:) Glory be to my Lord, the Most High.

The opening chapter of the Qur'an and any one other chapter are recited.

Islam in today's world Teacher's Resource Book   © John Murray

WORKSHEET 2.11

How a Muslim might grow closer to Allah

Help Nilufa of Al-Fatihah Educational Aids plan a course for Muslim parents, by completing the following matrix.

On this table, write summary notes for the middle column explaining how this aspect of revelation might develop a person's faith. The page references tell you where in the Student's Book you should look. Try to use and explain the key words in the third column.

Idea	How does this help Muslims to know Allah	Key words
The signs of Allah in the natural world	pages 29–31	Creating Sustaining
The role of the Qur'an	page 33	Comforting Guiding Warning
How Allah makes himself known through Muhammad ﷺ and the Hadith	page 32	Communicating Exemplifying (being an example)
How religious experience can lead a person to Allah	pages 34–5	Living Personal
The value of salah and other acts of ibadah e.g. sawm, Hajj, zakah	pages 12–13, 36–8	Closeness Submitting Obeying

© John Murray   *Islam in today's world Teacher's Resource Book*

WORKSHEET 2.12

Not such a perfect world?

Fill in the grid below to help you complete Activity 4 on page 40.

Source	Problem	Natural/Human-made suffering?	Explanation?
A			
B			
C			
D			
E			
F			

WORKSHEET 2.13

The story of the fall of humankind

This account has been simplified from Abdullah Yusuf Ali's translation of surah 2.30–39 into English. It is designed to help you with the Activity on page 43.

> And the Lord said to the angels, 'I will create a **vicegerent** on Earth.' They replied, 'Will you put someone on Earth who will cause mischief and trouble while we are praising and glorifying You?' to which the Lord said 'I know things which you cannot know.'
>
> So the Lord created Adam and taught him the name of everything on Earth. The Lord asked the angels to name everything too so that He could show them they did not know as much as they thought they did, saying, 'Didn't I tell you that I know the secrets of heaven and Earth; that I know what you reveal and what you conceal from me? Bow down to Adam!' So all the angels bowed down to Adam except Iblis, a jinn (later called Shaytan). He refused and was haughty, one of those who reject faith.
>
> The Lord said, 'O Adam, dwell with your wife in the Garden. You may eat any of the bountiful fruits there, as long as you never go near this one special tree. If you do, terrible things will happen to you.'
>
> But Shaytan made Adam and his wife Hawa slip out of the garden and away from the state of perfect happiness they had been living in. So, because they had done this, the Lord said to them, 'You must leave! You will live dutifully, you and all other people, on Earth. There will be difficulties between you.'
>
> Adam understood the truth of the Lord's words. So the Lord turned to him, because he is the Most Merciful, and said, 'Go down to Earth. I will give guidance to you. Whoever follows it should never fear or grieve. But I warn anyone who rejects their faith and ignores My guidance that they will become "Companions of the Fire" for ever!'
>
> **vicegerent** = someone who acts for someone else

Complete these sentences in your own words.

1. This story is about _____

2. Allah creates Adam because _____

3. Allah commanded all the angels to bow down before Adam because _____

4. One of the angels _____

5. Adam lived a perfect life in the Garden with Hawa, but then _____

6. Allah showed mercy to Adam and Hawa by _____

© John Murray — *Islam in today's world Teacher's Resource Book*

WORKSHEET 2.14

Why do people suffer?

Imran's story
My brother was thirteen when he started getting really sick. He went for lots of tests and was told he had leukaemia. The treatment made his hair fall out but all his mates at school were really good about it. No one took the mickey. It made things hard at home, though. Mum was so worried about Umar all the time she didn't have much time for the rest of us. We had to be good because she had so many other things to worry about and it wasn't normal.

My brother is getting better. His hair's coming back and he isn't so sick all the time. The doctors are pleased but it's still very scary. We don't know when things will be back to normal.

Shipa's story
Shipa was born with one leg. She has an artificial one which is covered up well by her shalwaar kameez, so lots of people at school don't even know. She only tells a few people: her year head, her PE teacher and her best friend all know. Other people seem to think she walks slowly because of her weight. Others don't notice.

It doesn't really bother her that much; she's used to it, but she wonders what will happen when it's time for her to get married. Will her parents find someone good who doesn't hold it against her, or will it put them off?

Ayesha's story
My Dad died nine months ago. We were sleeping when it happened, so no one told us until the morning. We came down into the kitchen and Mum was crying. My big brother was over from the shop. He had his hand on Mum's shoulder. 'It's Dad,' he said in a strange voice. 'He's been killed in a car crash.'

Dad's car had skidded on a patch of ice and crashed into a tree. The police reckoned he was trying to avoid hitting a pedestrian or an animal. I think that's true. My Dad was so kind-hearted he would have done his best not to hurt anyone.

Abdul Bari's story
I came to Britain (from Somalia) ten years ago so I was quite small but I remember the war there really well. Planes would fly over our house at night and the bombs and the shooting would keep us awake. When my uncle got killed my Dad decided it was time for us to leave. We left early in the morning, my mum, dad and four sisters. Life in Britain wasn't too great when we first came. We were in a hotel room for one year until they found us a proper house. Now we are happy. I like my school and my friends. I get to have my own bedroom 'cause I'm the only boy! We still have family in Somalia. They tell us that things are better. I want to go back when I am sixteen years old.

In groups or as a class, complete the following tasks.

1. Make a list of the people who suffered in each of the stories. Explain in what way they suffered.
2. Try to think of what good, if any, might have come from the story.
3. Think of three questions you would ask one of the storytellers if you had the opportunity to meet them. What answers do you think they might give?
4. On your own, complete the following sentences:

I was moved by _____'s story. When I read it I felt _____

_____

I think I felt like that because _____

_____

I think another person might have different feelings if they read it because _____

_____

WORKSHEET 2.15 sheet 1

How might Muslims answer those who say there is no God?

Use this sheet to help you prepare your answers to the review task on page 46.

Objection	Response – ideas you could use	Pages of Units 1 and 2
I have not heard or seen God. If God exists, surely I would have heard from him by now?	• Allah has spoken through creation • Allah has sent prophets • Allah has spoken through the Qur'an • Fitrah • Taqwa	29–31 32–3 32–3 29 37
There is too much suffering in this world	• Allah is merciful and compassionate • Suffering may be Allah's will • Suffering comes from free will • This life is not the only life • Good can come out of suffering	2 42 43 44 45
Science and modern ideas have disproved religion	• Islam is the natural way – a practical religion • Allah is beyond science and human understanding • Certain things can only be known by special revelation from Allah	5 24, 26, 28 32–3
The people who follow God are not a good advertisement for him	• Muslims are ordinary human beings. They make mistakes too • You shouldn't look at the followers but at Allah. It is Allah whom Muslims worship • Many Muslims are working to make this world a better place	20–22 7, 25 18–22

© John Murray   *Islam in today's world Teacher's Resource Book*   47

WORKSHEET 2.15 sheet 2

How might Muslims answer those who say there is no God?

Choose one of the speakers on page 46. You can use this writing frame to help you write your reply. Include one or two of the ideas on the previous page to complete this letter. Use your own words, but remember you are writing from a Muslim perspective.

Dear _____

You say _____
_____
_____

I can understand how you feel. I have felt like that at times as well. But my religion has taught me to hold firm in my belief in Allah.

The most important thing it teaches me about this is that _____
_____
_____
_____
_____
_____

It also teaches me that _____
_____
_____
_____
_____

The result of these beliefs is that _____
_____
_____
_____
_____

What I say may not change your views but I do hope it shows you why, as a Muslim, I feel so sure about Allah.

Yours

Islam in today's world Teacher's Resource Book © John Murray

WORKSHEET 2.16

Examination practice: Thinking about Allah

Suffering and evil

As you answer this question, use only information on Islam.

1 How do the existence of both suffering and evil in the world challenge a person's belief in God? (6)

2 'The fact that suffering and evil exist proves that there is no God.' How would a religious believer reply to this statement? (8)

3 Do you think that having a belief in God can help people cope with suffering in their lives? Explain your view. (6)

NEAB, Specimen paper 1997, 1998

WORKSHEET 2.17

Qur'an file cards: Thinking about Allah

Reference: Surah 1
Student's Book: Page 1
Name of surah: Al-Fatihah (The Opening)
Summary: Muslim beliefs about Allah; the relationship of Muslims to Allah
Application: What Muslims believe; reason why Muslims have faith

THINKING ABOUT ALLAH

Reference: Surah 6.48
Student's Book: Page 32
Name of surah: Al-An'am (The Cattle)
Summary: Prophets are sent to tell people the good about Allah's existence and to warn people that they are accountable to Him
Application: Belief

THINKING ABOUT ALLAH

Reference: Surah 2.177
Student's Book: Page 3
Name of surah: Al-Baqarah (The Heifer/Cow)
Summary: Key Muslim beliefs, how Muslims should live their lives
Application: What Muslims believe

THINKING ABOUT ALLAH

Reference: Surah 2.2
Student's Book: Page 32
Name of surah: Al-Baqarah (The Heifer/Cow)
Summary: The Qu'ran should be accepted as the Truth. It is a guide to life which come directly from Allah
Application: Status of Qu'ran, belief

THINKING ABOUT ALLAH

Reference: Surah 6.103
Student's Book: Page 26
Name of surah: Al-An'am (The Cattle)
Summary: Allah understands everything, yet is beyond human understanding
Application: Nature of Allah, transcendence of Allah

THINKING ABOUT ALLAH

Reference: Surah 5.3-4
Student's Book: Page 33
Name of surah: Al-Ma'idah (The Repast/Meal)
Summary: Islam is the perfect religion, chosen for people by Allah
Application: Prophecy

THINKING ABOUT ALLAH

Reference: Surah 112.1-4
Student's Book: Page 24
Name of surah: Al-Ikhlas (Purity of Faith)
Summary: Belief in Tawhid, the Oneness of Allah, Allah has no son
Application: Nature of Allah, belief

THINKING ABOUT ALLAH

Reference: Surah 107.4-7
Student's Book: Page 37
Name of surah: Al-Ma'un (The Neighbourly Assistance)
Summary: People who do not pray or pray just for show and do not help less fortunate neighbours will be punished by Allah
Application: Worship, prayer, pillars; importance of prayer in Islam

THINKING ABOUT ALLAH

Reference: Surah 50.6-7
Student's Book: Page 30
Name of surah: Qaf ('Q')
Summary: The existence of the universe is a proof of the existence of Allah
Application: Creation, environment

THINKING ABOUT ALLAH

Reference: Surah 50.16
Student's Book: Page 28
Name of surah: Qaf ('Q')
Summary: Allah is closer to a person than their jugular vein
Application: Nature of Allah, immanence of Allah, belief

THINKING ABOUT ALLAH

WORKSHEET 2.18

End of Unit Quiz: Thinking about Allah

Test yourself or your neighbour with this quick quiz.

1. What belief is summed up in surah 112 of the Qur'an?
2. True or false? Islam is polytheistic.
3. What does the word *Islam* mean?
4. What is *Tawhid*?
5. Explain why Muslim artists might use calligraphy in their paintings.
6. State one of the 99 names of Allah, and explain what this name suggests about Allah.
7. What does the *transcendence of Allah* mean?
8. Give one example of *general revelation* in Islam.
9. Give one example of *special revelation* in Islam.
10. What is *Fitrah*?
11. What is the role of a prophet in Islam?
12. Why do Muslims see the Qur'an as the most important source of revelation?
13. What is a *revert*?
14. How many times a day are Muslims expected to perform salah?
15. Explain one way in which salah helps Muslims in their daily lives.
16. What is a Sufi?
17. What is the difference between natural suffering and human-made suffering?
18. Who is Shaytan? Explain one thing that Shaytan does.
19. 'Muslims believe in original sin.' True or false?
20. What might a Muslim mean when they say 'suffering is a test'?

UNIT 3

Issues of life and death

Overview

The introductory investigation (3.1) focuses on the key ideas for this unit – beliefs about the sanctity of life, death and life after death. Then separate investigations apply these ideas to the moral issues of abortion (3.2), euthanasia (3.3), and capital punishment (3.4). The unit also investigates how beliefs about death may affect the living, and how issues about the quality of life may alter the way we feel about these three topics.

These issues of life and death are topics on which students may have strongly-held opinions. It is good to emphasise to students from the start that to get the highest marks for evaluative writing in the examination (and to avoid becoming that self-opinionated relative whose visits they dread!), they must be able to recognise that some people have different opinions from them. They must be able to explain not only their own view but also those views of people who have the opposite opinion. They should also be able to support their opinion. Only then can they expose the weaknesses in their opponents' arguments and uphold the strengths in their own.

Some teachers have a favourite excerpt from Prime Minister's question-time which they use to illustrate this point, but a carefully-staged argument in class on a topic on which students feel passionately can make the same point.

It is worth remembering that when dealing with issues of life and death, there could be students in your classroom who have had recent personal experience of death. Teachers may also have strong views on these issues, but must ensure that they maintain a position that makes it possible for students to hold a different one.

3.1 What do Muslims believe about life and death?

Pages 48–9

The sanctity of life

ACTIVITY A explores the issue of the sanctity of life, first individually and then as a group activity. Ensure that this opinion-gathering exercise remains anonymous, to encourage students to be free in their responses.
Worksheet 3.1 is a time-saving sheet to support this activity.
Worksheet 3.2 will help students develop their evaluative writing by encouraging them to recognise differing opinions on the sanctity of life.

Pages 50–51

This spread features a Muslim woman from East London who works for the family business, Taslim Funerals.

In our interview with her, Moona talked freely about people's attitude to death and dead bodies. Text in the 'bubbles' could provoke useful classroom discussion. Activities 1 and 2 provide starters for those discussions, but teachers should extend the questions to follow the issues raised by their students.

If classroom discussion is impossible, **Worksheet 3.3** provides a written task to get students thinking about Moona's views. It could be used as homework.

Page 52

The Checkpoint explains Muslim beliefs about judgement. Students need to be clear about this teaching because it underpins much of what Muslims say about death, and it has an impact on many aspects of life too.
Worksheet 3.4 supports the task on page 52. This can be extended by:

a) blocking out some of the text in column 1 so that students have to provide the explanation as well as the application

b) adding a further 'honesty' column: 'A statement I would make in this situation'.

3.2 Can abortion ever be justified?

This investigation is structured entirely around a true case that happened some years ago. Sumayah (a pseudonym) is a young Muslim woman who faced an agonising decision about whether to have an abortion.

Page 53

SAVE AS ... In real life, Sumayah did decide to have an abortion.
CHECKPOINT If you need further information about how abortion is carried out, see the *Christianity in today's world* Teacher's Resource Book, page 26.

Pages 54–5

This decision flow chart may be somewhat artificial – such decisions are not taken in such a linear way in real life – but it tries to isolate the different questions that contribute to the final decision. It could have greater impact if you do not study the Student's Book first but unfold the decisions, one by one, in a classroom discussion or simulation.

UNIT 3

3.3 Why is euthanasia forbidden in Islam?

It is immediately clear from the title to this investigation that this issue is in a different category from abortion. Abortion is a matter of relative morality for Muslims, whereas euthanasia in Islam is an absolute. So the style of this investigation is necessarily different. Rather than deciding, the emphasis is on understanding and explaining a decision which Allah takes for Muslims. This is the reason for introducing a non-Muslim case study – to create a dynamic between Muslim belief and the life of non-Muslims.

Page 56
CHECKPOINT Many people quote the Netherlands as a country where euthanasia is legal. This is not strictly true. Euthanasia remains illegal, in theory. But there are careful legal guidelines laid down for doctors and if these are followed doctors **are not prosecuted** for carrying out euthanasia. See *Christianity in today's world* Student's Book page 21 for an example and an explanation.

3.4 Is it ever right to kill a human being as a punishment?

When a particularly horrible crime is committed, especially if the victim is a child, then the call is for a return to the death penalty. However, a double standard applies regarding outsiders' perceptions of countries where the application of Shari'ah means that capital punishment is a possibility. Capital punishment is then presented as barbaric, an offence against human rights. Islamic punishment is stereotyped as rigid and vengeful, when in fact a great emphasis lies on mercy and reconciliation. So this investigation steps into interesting yet controversial territory. The aim of this investigation is to guide students through the issues step by step while allowing plenty of opportunity for passionate yet informed debate.

This investigation begins with a series of real cases which took place in 1999. Some teachers may prefer to begin with more topical cases of serious crime.

Page 61
ACTIVITY B Worksheet 3.7 supports this activity.
CHECKPOINT Students need to understand the terms listed here. Teachers may like to ask students to write out the seven headings, with a definition in their own words.

Involvement of the victim's family in the fate of offenders
This is not part of the British legal system, although occasionally victims are involved in the rehabilitation of offenders. It was this aspect of the Gilford case that provoked the long controversy in 1998 when Frank Gilford was accused of profiting from his sister's death for accepting compensation in lieu of capital punishment. In fact, having settled his legal costs, he donated most of the remaining money to a hospital to set up a children's unit in memory of his sister.
ACTIVITY B provides an opportunity for students to explore this issue.

Page 62
ACTIVITY Worksheet 3.8 supports this activity, which begins by inviting students to respond personally to the issues surrounding capital punishment. Students could compare their responses to the **Save As . . .** task 4 and their attitude to capital punishment revealed in the activity on page 60 at the beginning of this investigation. If their attitude has changed at all, why do they think this is? The activity will lead naturally into a debate on capital punishment. **Worksheet 3.8** can also be used to set up a debate on the issue of capital punishment:

1. Give one statement to each student or group of students.
2. Ask them to base their arguments in the debate around this point and to argue it as strongly as possible.
3. Students must stick to the viewpoint they have been given, whether they agree or not. Allow time at the end for them to state their own views openly.

Page 63
FOCUS TASK Having explored the Islamic principles of punishment, students are now asked to use their understanding. They are asked to write a letter to their MP in the role of a Muslim. This activity is supported by a writing frame on **Worksheet 3.9**. In recent years Members of Parliament have been given a free vote on this issue. You might like to invite your local MP to discuss how they voted, or would vote given the chance. You could also show your MP the results of the Focus Task.

Worksheet 3.10 is a light-hearted exercise in public speaking. Clearly some students will find this more of a challenge than others, and teachers will need to decide whether or not to allow students to use their notes.

The value of debates and this sort of exercise cannot be over-estimated. It is well known that explaining yourself to others can really help clarify your own ideas. If classes are not used to this sort of activity, you could start by allowing the exercise to take place in small groups.

One person in each group will need to act as the chairperson, ensuring that the appointed person is allowed to speak for one minute, uninterrupted. Likewise, groups who are not used to class debates can be prepared by small group debates, but again with a chairperson who must ensure that *everyone* speaks.

Page 64
The Review Task provides an opportunity for students to use what they have learnt in an examination-style question. It deliberately uses the same questions as the equivalent in *Christianity in today's world*. **Worksheets 3.11**, **3.12** and **3.13** again have quotation cards, examination practice and an end of unit quiz.

WORKSHEET 3.1

The sanctity of life

1. Choose four of the sentences below to complete.
2. Cut them out along the dotted lines.
3. Complete each sentence in your own way.
4. Write the letter of the sentence (a–i), but not your name, on the back.
5. As a class, sort the sentences into categories using the letters on the back. Then discuss each other's ideas.

a) The value of life is

b) Life is sacred because

c) My life is worth

d) Life is

e) Humans are precious because

f) Humans are priceless because

g) A baby is precious because

h) Regarding the sanctity of life, I think

i) Human life is/is not more valuable than animal life because

WORKSHEET 3.2 sheet 1

The sanctity of life

You are going to make a display which illustrates Muslim beliefs about the sanctity of life.

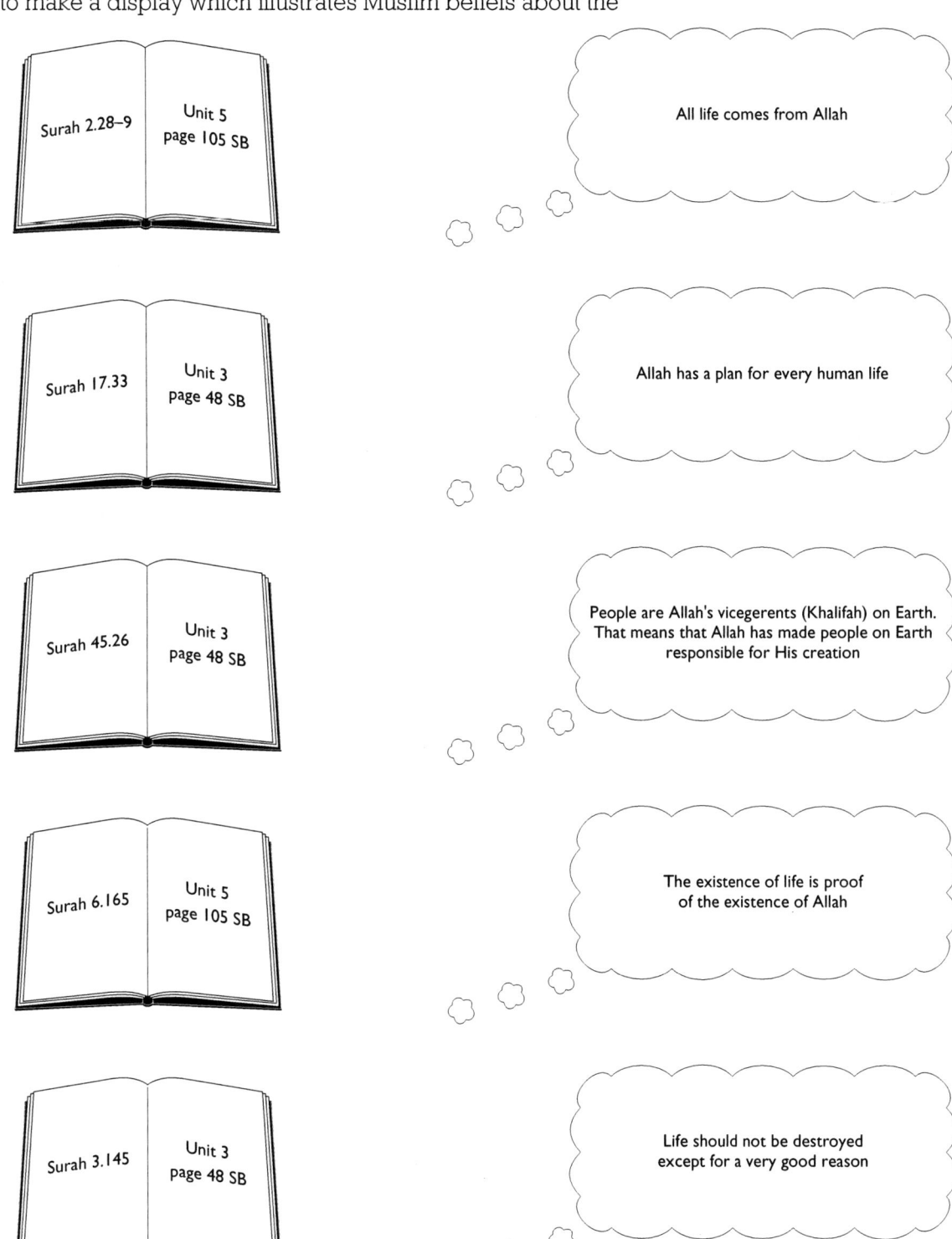

| Surah 2.28–9 | Unit 5 page 105 SB | | All life comes from Allah |

| Surah 17.33 | Unit 3 page 48 SB | | Allah has a plan for every human life |

| Surah 45.26 | Unit 3 page 48 SB | | People are Allah's vicegerents (Khalifah) on Earth. That means that Allah has made people on Earth responsible for His creation |

| Surah 6.165 | Unit 5 page 105 SB | | The existence of life is proof of the existence of Allah |

| Surah 3.145 | Unit 3 page 48 SB | | Life should not be destroyed except for a very good reason |

1. Look up the five passages from the Qur'an. They can also be found in your textbook on the pages indicated.
2. Match each reference to one of the beliefs in the bubbles. The quote from the Qur'an should support the belief in the bubble.
3. Put the pairs on a large sheet of paper but don't stick them until you have done **sheet 2**.
Now turn to sheet 2.

WORKSHEET 3.2 sheet 2

The sanctity of life

Each of the statements below relates to the sanctity of life. Match each of these statements to one of the beliefs and add them to your display.

1. Cut out these statements.
2. Sort them into two piles:
   a) those that you think a Muslim would say, and
   b) those that you think a Muslim would not say.
3. Match those in pile **a)** to a teaching on your large sheet of paper to make a sanctity of life display.
4. Draw or stick five faces onto the display. Give each person a thought bubble containing the belief and Qur'an passage and a speech bubble with their statements.
5. Write a paragraph entitled: 'My views on the sanctity of life' and add it to the display.

Human beings *must* make sure animals are not mistreated	When I saw my baby brother born, I knew there was a God
Human life is a miracle in itself	I will die when it is my time to die
All babies are a gift from Allah	Large companies should not be allowed to pollute our water supply
It is wrong to murder another human being	I will only resort to killing pests when every other method has failed
I am not afraid of death	The human body is a miracle of design

WORKSHEET 3.3

Meet Moona

Moona Taslim-Saif works for Taslim Funerals in East London. How would she answer these questions? Use pages 50–51 to help you.

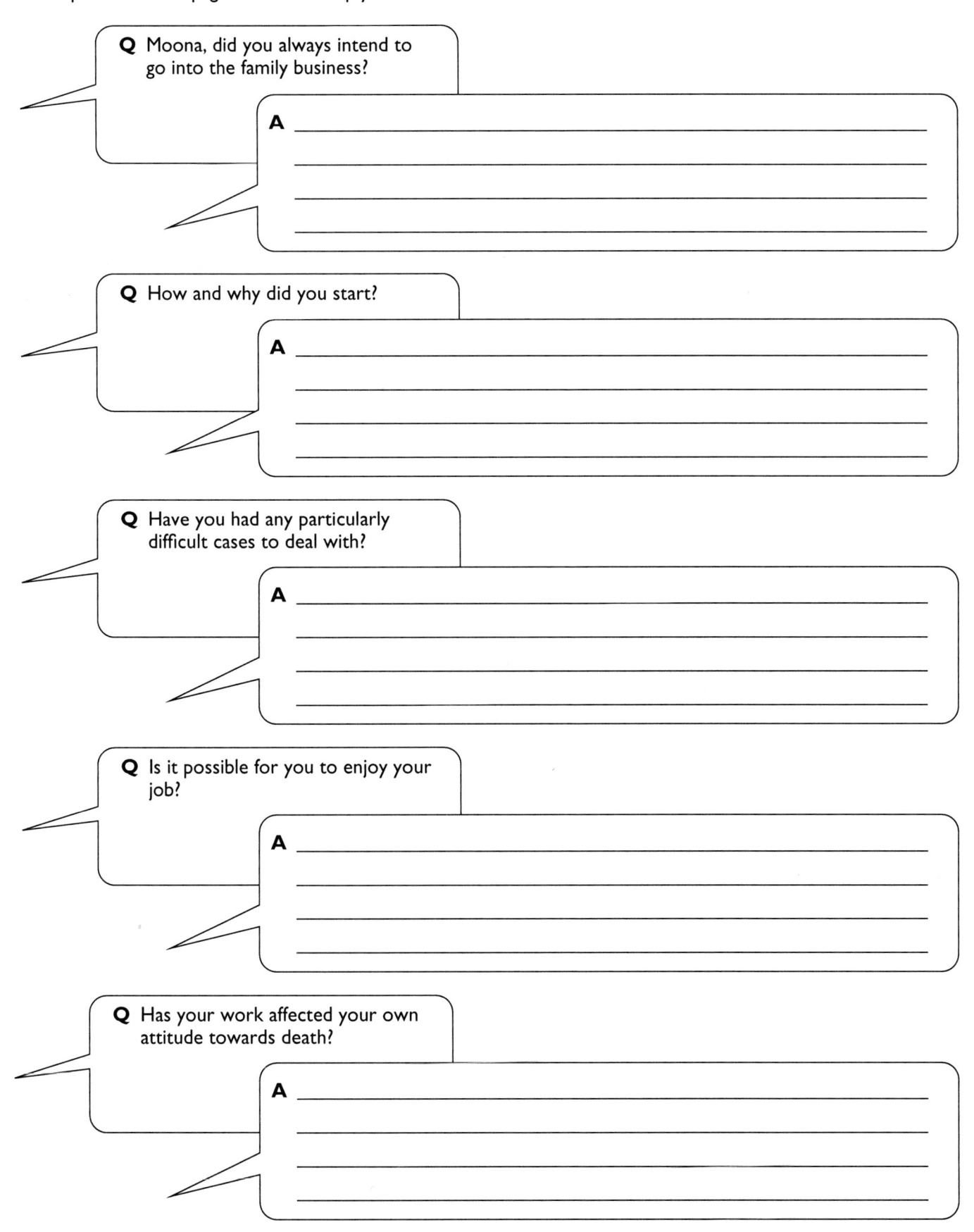

Q Moona, did you always intend to go into the family business?

A _____

Q How and why did you start?

A _____

Q Have you had any particularly difficult cases to deal with?

A _____

Q Is it possible for you to enjoy your job?

A _____

Q Has your work affected your own attitude towards death?

A _____

WORKSHEET 3.4

How do beliefs about life and death affect yourself and others?

Complete the following chart to show the way that these beliefs might affect people.

The possible effect of believing in life after death and the Day of Judgement on your attitudes to …	On your actions …	Impact of these actions on other people
Bereavement It helps you to cope with death because you know there is the life to come	At my grandfather's funeral, I …	The believer …
Honesty It stops you being dishonest because you know Allah sees everything you do and will judge you for it	When I found a purse on a train …	
Possessions It makes you realise that material possessions are temporary and not the source of true happiness	When I look for a job …	
Suffering It gives you the determination to rise above problems in this life because you know life is a test	When my life is hard, I …	
Personal responsibility It forces you to think about people other than yourself and your responsibilities towards the whole of creation	When deciding what to do with my leisure time, I …	

WORKSHEET 3.5

Sumayah's choice

Here is a conversation between Sumayah and her uncle.

1 Write what you think Sumayah should do on the first line.
2 Use the Student's Book to help you fill in what Sumayah might say in the missing parts of the conversation. Make sure she explains her reasons.

Sumayah: Uncle. I've made my decision. I'm going to _____

(Explain whether you will have the baby or have an abortion)

Uncle: So how did you come to that decision, Sumayah? Be sure you have thought through all the issues.
Sumayah: I've tried to do that.
Uncle: Tell me about it. What does the Qur'an say that is relevant to abortion?
Sumayah: It says _____

_____

_____

_____

Uncle: And how about what scholars have to say about this?
Sumayah: Some say abortion is permissible. Others do not. They disagree about when life begins. Some say _____

_____

Others say _____

_____

Uncle: What else did you consider?
Sumayah: The most important question seemed to be whether a baby being born badly deformed was a 'just cause' for abortion. I felt that _____

_____

_____

Uncle: Did you also consider the effect your decision would have on the rest of the family?
Sumayah: Yes of course, Uncle. I thought about _____

_____

_____

Uncle: I hope you thought about Akhirah (life after death).
Sumayah: That was on my mind the whole time because _____

_____

_____

Uncle: I see you have been thinking clearly, Sumayah. As-Salamu alaykum, my dear niece. I will ask Allah for His peace and blessing on you all.
Sumayah: My dear Uncle, thank you. Wa alaykum Salam!

© John Murray   *Islam in today's world Teacher's Resource Book*

WORKSHEET 3.6

Why must we suffer?

Write a dialogue between a Muslim and Annie Lindsell (you can read her story on page 58 of the Student's Book). She has a wasting disease and wants to choose when to die. She is not a Muslim, and knows nothing of Muslim beliefs.

In the conversation below you need to explain how a Muslim might view her situation.

Presenter: Tonight on 'Face to Face', pro-euthanasia campaigner Annie Lindsell is face to face with _____ from AMC, a Muslim group who oppose euthanasia. Over to you, Annie:

Annie: I am terminally ill. Doctors expect me to live only a few more months. I want the right to choose when to die. What is the Muslim attitude to that?

Muslim: I understand that you are in a lot of pain. I am sorry. However, the Muslim view on euthanasia is _____

Annie: Why do you believe that?

Muslim: We have many reasons. One of the most important is _____

Another is _____

Annie: I thought religion is supposed to help people who are suffering? How can your religion help me to cope with my situation?

Muslim: It can help give you a different angle on your suffering. Islam teaches that _____

(Explain the Muslim view that Allah has a plan)

It also teaches that _____

(Explain the Muslim view that good can come out of suffering)

In your situation this could mean that _____

(Explain how this could happen in Annie's life)

Annie: So is it a part of Allah's plan for me to suffer?

Muslim: Maybe. Suffering is _____

(Explain the Muslim view that suffering is a test)

Annie: Your God sounds rather cruel.

Muslim: Not at all. Even if we cannot understand Allah's plan, the Qur'an describes Allah as _____

which means that in your situation _____

Presenter: And there we'll have to leave it, I'm afraid. I'd like to thank both of our guests for coming this evening. You've given us a great many things to think about!

Islam in today's world Teacher's Resource Book   © John Murray

WORKSHEET 3.7

Islam and capital punishment

Draw a line from the point about capital punishment to the words in this quotation from the Qur'an (Surah 2.178–9) which state that view. You could highlight or underline the words in different colours to make it clearer. The first one has been done for you.

a) If someone murders they should be killed in return.

b) The family of the victim can spare the murderer and prevent the death sentence being carried out.

c) Capital punishment is an effective deterrent against murder.

> O you who believe!
> The Law of Equality is prescribed to you in cases of murder ...
> But if any remission is made by the brother of the slain,
> Then grant any reasonable demand
> And compensate him with handsome gratitude.
> This is a concession and a Mercy from your Lord.
> After this, whoever exceeds the limits
> Shall be in grave penalty ...
>
> In the Law of Equality there is saving of Life to you,
> O men of understanding;
> That you may restrain yourselves ...

d) A murderer who is spared the death penalty must pay compensation instead.

e) Capital punishment helps people to develop self-control.

f) Allah is forgiving and so allows for compensation to be paid instead.

WORKSHEET 3.8

What is your view on capital punishment?

1 Cut out each of the statements below.
2 On a large piece of paper (A3 or bigger), draw a scale like the one below, but much larger.
3 As a group, try to agree where to place each statement.
4 On your own, re-read all of the statements and choose the two that you agree with most strongly, and the two you disagree with most strongly. Use these to write two paragraphs explaining your own attitude to capital punishment.
5 a) Which of the statements could have been made by a Muslim?
  b) Which would definitely not be made by a Muslim?
  Support your answers with evidence from pages 60–61 of the Student's Book.

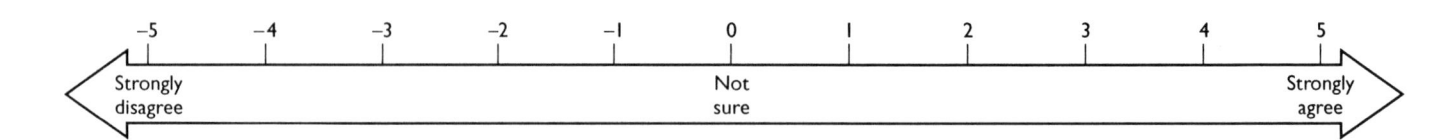

```
-5    -4    -3    -2    -1    0    1    2    3    4    5
Strongly                        Not                    Strongly
disagree                        sure                   agree
```

- If someone kills, they should be killed in return.

- What is the point of capital punishment? Killing the killer is not going to bring the victim back to life

- No legal system is perfect; mistakes are made and people are occasionally wrongly convicted. If capital punishment was allowed then an innocent person would sometimes be killed.

- I am opposed to capital punishment. Any punishment for a crime should aim to reform that person. We should never say that a person is beyond help.

- Capital punishment is a good deterrent. If you know you might be hanged, you'll think twice before killing someone.

- People have to be protected from killers. The only way to be sure that a killer won't kill again is to end their life.

- Capital punishment doesn't work as a deterrent: look at the countries where they allow the death penalty – there are still plenty of murders.

- I am not sure that capital punishment is such a good punishment for murder. It must be a greater punishment to the killer's family than to the killer themselves.

- If we allow capital punishment, that makes us as bad as the killer. Retribution is just another name for revenge, and that should not be allowed in a civilised society.

- Some murders are more serious than others. For example, murders of police officers should be treated differently from where a husband murders his wife or vice versa.

- I believe that any killing is wrong, including capital punishment.

- Capital punishment saves money. Life imprisonment puts too much financial pressure on a country. Why should tax-payers have to give money for criminals?

- Capital punishment gives a clear message that a society totally disapproves of murder.

- Some murderers would prefer death to life imprisonment. Death is too easy a punishment. People who do terrible things will suffer more if they are imprisoned for life.

WORKSHEET 3.9

A letter to your local MP

> 4 Cyprus Way
> Masingstone
> Herks   MS3 4TD
>
> 25 February 2001
>
> Dear . . . .
>
> I understand that you have been appointed to a special committee in Parliament looking at the death penalty in this country. Well done! As someone who has lived in your constituency for many years I am writing to you to make sure that you understand the Muslim perspective on this issue. Many of your voters at the next election will be Muslim. I hope you agree it's important that you consider our beliefs in any discussions you might have about capital punishment.
>
> The Islamic approach to capital punishment is based on Shari'ah. Shari'ah is _____
> _____
> _____
>
> *(Explain what Shari'ah means and how it is worked out)*
>
> The Qur'an, which is the highest source of authority for Muslims, supports the use of capital punishment in certain cases. For example, _____
> _____
> _____
> _____
>
> *(Give at least two examples, with reasons if possible)*
>
> Islam also teaches that it is very important to be merciful. In cases where a person is found guilty, we believe _____
> _____
> _____
>
> *(Explain how compensation might allow mercy, and how mercy might be rewarded)*
>
> There are other factors affecting Muslim beliefs about capital punishment, including
> _____
> _____
>
> *(Explain at least two other factors)*
>
> Some aspects of the Islamic system of punishment might be useful in Britain, for example _____
> _____
> _____
>
> *(Suggest some examples)*
>
> I realise that you will have many letters from your constituents on this controversial topic but I hope that you will not ignore the help that knowledge of Islam can bring you. Yours sincerely
>
> . . . .

© John Murray — *Islam in today's world Teacher's Resource Book*

WORKSHEET 3.10

Just a minute: life issues

Note to teachers:
1. Copy and cut out the statements on this sheet.
2. Give each student one of the statements.
3. Ask the students to prepare notes that will enable them to speak in support of their statement for at least a minute, with no pauses! They should try to include relevant Islamic teachings or ideas too. If they disagree with the statement it should not matter – they can put their own views afterwards.

• Victims of crime should have a say in the punishment of the offenders.	• People are responsible for their own actions. They will be judged on them after death.
• It is wrong to use animals for medical experiments.	• Making something legal doesn't make it morally acceptable.
• Everything in this life is guided by the purpose of Allah.	• Life is a gift from Allah who is the source of all life.
• Life begins when the soul enters the body.	• Death is not the end.
• It is always wrong to kill.	• Life is a test.
• Animals do not have the same rights as human beings.	• No severer of the womb-relationship ties will ever enter paradise.
• Humans should not poison their bodies with tobacco or drugs.	• Euthanasia is never morally acceptable.

WORKSHEET 3.11

Examination practice: Issues of life and death

Abortion

As you answer this question use information on Islam wherever appropriate.

A pregnant woman has been told that she will have a severely disabled child. She is advised to consider an abortion.

a) i) Explain why believers in one religious tradition are against abortion in the situation outlined above. (5)

ii) Explain why believers in one religious tradition think that abortion may be justified in the same situation. (4)

b) State and explain **two** circumstances, **other than the one above**, when abortion is regarded by some religious believers as acceptable. (6)

c) 'If a baby is not wanted by its mother there are many people who would adopt it. It should not be killed' Do you agree? Give reasons for your answer, showing that you have thought about more than one point of view. (5)

NEAB, 1998

WORKSHEET 3.12

Qur'an file cards: Issues of life and death

Reference: Surah 3.145
Student's Book: Page 48
Name of surah: Al-Imran (The family of Imran)
Summary: Allah determines the time of death
Application: Suicide, capital punishment, euthanasia

Reference: Surah 22.5
Student's Book: Page 54
Name of surah: Al-Hajj (The Pilgrimage)
Summary: Human beings are created from dust, then sperm. This develops into something that looks like a leech, then into a partly formed body. This stays in the womb for the right time and is then born as a baby
Application: Creation, abortion, sanctity of life

Reference: Surah 17.33
Student's Book: Page 48
Name of surah: Al-Isra' (the Night Journey)
Summary: Life is created by Allah and should not be taken away without just cause
Application: Capital punishment, euthanasia, abortion

Reference: Surah 2.153-6
Student's Book: Page 57
Name of surah: Al-Baqarah (The Heifer/Cow)
Summary: Life is a test. Patience will be rewarded by Allah
Application: Suffering, purpose of life, sanctity of life

Reference: Surah 45.26
Student's Book: Page 48
Name of surah: Al-Jathiya (The Kneeling Down)
Summary: Allah gives life and Allah takes it away, so Allah will judge how a person used that life
Application: Death, judgement

Reference: Surah 2.178-9
Student's Book: Page 61
Name of surah: Al-Baqarah (The Heifer/Cow)
Summary: Law of Equality (life for life) in punishing murder will reduce loss of life
Application: Capital punishment

WORKSHEET 3.13

End of Unit Quiz: Issues of life and death

Test yourself or your neighbour with this quick quiz.

1. What does the phrase *sanctity of life* mean?
2. Write out one passage from the Qur'an that might be used by Muslims to show that life is sacred.
3. State two things that Muslims believe will happen on the Day of Judgement.
4. What is *ensoulment*?
5. Give two different Muslim views on when ensoulment takes place.
6. What is *niyyah*?
7. How might niyyah figure in a decision on abortion?
8. Explain the difference between *voluntary* and *involuntary* euthanasia.
9. Are voluntary or involuntary euthanasia acceptable within Islam?
10. State one Muslim teaching that is used to argue against euthanasia.
11. What is a *hospice*?
12. Why might Muslims in Britain today be less likely to use a hospice than non-Muslims?
13. Define *zulm*.
14. What is *capital punishment*?
15. The Qur'an approves capital punishment. True or false?
16. Give examples of how the principle of mercy affects the Muslim approach to capital punishment.

UNIT 4

Relationships

Overview

The first three spreads are an introductory investigation (4.1) exploring the core idea for this unit of ummah – the caring community to which all Muslims belong. We then investigate three topics: sex, marriage and divorce (4.2), gender equality (4.3), and racial prejudice and discrimination (4.4).

Within some specifications, 'Relationships' also includes the topic of the 'Individual in society', which we have covered in Unit 1 (pages 18–22).

Relationships can be a challenge to teach, not least because at Key Stage 4 the interests of boys and girls can differ greatly. In our experience, boys are less keen than girls to spend time talking about love and marriage. This may in turn result in poor answers to examination questions about relationships. Teachers therefore need to think carefully about keeping the boys on track throughout this unit.

Starting strategies

Page 65
As in other units, we begin with a quote. However, there are many other starting points including the 'Relationships web' from the *Christianity in today's world* Student's Book page 33, which can be used without adaptation in this context.

4.1 Ummah – the caring community

This introductory investigation explores three expressions of the Muslim ummah: Hajj, the mosque, and the family.

You might want to use a large class spider diagram to build up a visual representation of the various levels of the meaning of ummah over the next six pages.

The united community

The emphasis in pages 66–7 is on unity. It is interesting to note that in our discussions with faith community advisers on this book, this spread came in for particular attention. Worldwide unity of Islam is a fine idea but one that is hard to achieve in practice. Nationalist tendencies often prevail. Even at Hajj, pilgrims break largely into national groups.

Pages 66–7
ACTIVITY The Christian Education Movement's video on Hajj, even though it is now quite old, can still be used to supplement the pictures in Source A. On the video, Muslims can be seen doing all the things shown in Source A. With careful use of the 'pause' button you may even catch the expressions on pilgrims' faces and be able to ask students, 'What do you think he/she is feeling now?' ... 'Why does doing that make him/her feel that way?'

Worksheet 4.1 supports this task with or without the video.

Pages 68–9

The praying community: Life at the mosque

Many students will have studied the mosque at Key Stage 3, so this investigation can build on their existing knowledge and understanding by looking at the role of the mosque in the community. If students have not studied the mosque before, or if they cannot recall basic information, teachers may need to recap, perhaps using a video such as *A guide to the Mosque and Id ul-Fitr* or the section on 'The Mosque' in the *Believe it or not* series.

You may choose to visit a mosque as a part of this unit (see page 12 in this book for ideas about this). You need to prepare the staff at the mosque for the needs of a GCSE group. The students need to learn about the role of the mosque in the community, and not simply the features of the mosque. A good visit may involve a Muslim talking about how they feel the mosque encourages Muslims not only to pray, but also to feel part of the ummah, the worldwide family of Muslims. The following checklist might be useful to help prepare a potential speaker.

How do the following help Muslims to feel part of the ummah?

- Salah and the call to prayer
- Jumu'ah prayers
- The khutbah (talk given by the imam on Fridays)
- The imam
- Support provided in the mosque for people getting married or when someone dies, or at other times of need
- Any meetings, of small and large groups, that take place in the mosque
- Teaching of Arabic, community languages, about Islam
- Charitable work initiated at the mosque
- Festival celebrations, especially Id ul-Adha and Id ul-Fitr
- Activities in the mosque during Ramadan, e.g. itikaf, breaking the fast

This list might also guide you in leading class discussion around the illustration on pages 68–9.
ACTIVITY The visual here is loosely modelled on the Islamic Cultural Centre and Central London Mosque in Regent's Park. At the time of writing, their website was

UNIT 4

under construction but it was already helpful. Its address is: www.islamic-centre.org.uk/ Students could visit this website as part of the first question in the Activity.

Worksheet 4.2 will support less able students in completing Activity 2.

Pages 70–71
The nurturing community: The family

The Checkpoint explains a key idea for this investigation: the Muslim regards 'family' as the extended family.

An interesting discussion might focus on the impact on family life and young children when both parents work. Some primary schools in Britain report that grandparents are increasingly involved in the delivery and collection of children from school – an arrangement that relies on extended families living close to each other. Students could share their views on the advantages and disadvantages of extended family involvement in this and other areas of life. How can members of extended families support each other?

This spread is inevitably idealised in its view of family life, and many students in your class will be able to paint a very different picture, either from their own experience or from what they see on TV. Teachers need to ask questions that make it possible for students to voice both positive and negative experiences of family life.

4.2 Why do Muslims say people should marry?

Muslims are expected to get married. The overall aim of this investigation is to explain and understand this expectation. It is not a random regulation but is crucial to the whole Muslim view of the structure of society. The family is the foundation on which the rest of society is built. Teaching about sex and divorce supports marriage and gives a high status to marriage. From the start it is vital that students appreciate the centrality of marriage to Muslim expectations.

Page 72
The opening activity is a light-hearted issue-raiser to balance some of the heavier material to come.

An alternative starting point beginning from a more Muslim perspective will be found on **Worksheet 4.3** which allows students to compare the qualities of an ideal partner with the view of a group of Muslims who were attempting to base their ideas on the principles of the Qur'an and the Sunnah.

Page 74
Arranged marriage

Not all Muslims have arranged marriages. It is a cultural rather than a religious phenomenon. However, where it does take place, arranged marriage is widely misunderstood by non-Muslims in Britain. It is often treated with patronising disdain or cynicism, and portrayed in a stereotypical manner. Our aim on this spread is to challenge those stereotypes. Arranged marriages take different forms; they are often very successful; they are arranged within a set of precedents and traditions designed to ensure compatibility.

A range of views on the subject are represented in the Activity, which provides a starting point for students to explore the idea.

Where students have little or no understanding of the idea, it may be interesting to begin with a brainstorm on what they think the term 'arranged marriage' means and how it is different from a 'marriage based on falling in love'. Point out that there are many approaches to arranged marriage. Parents are involved to varying degrees in 'arranging' their child's marriage in nearly all cultures. You could draw a line representing the extremes between an instant marriage after a whirlwind holiday romance, and an arranged marriage that takes place without the bride and groom seeing each other before the ceremony (which is very rare in the Muslim community in Britain today, and arguably non-Islamic). They can place other marriages that they know about on the line between these extremes. Where, for instance, would they place the latest royal wedding?

Page 75
Question 1: This is ideal for class discussion.
Worksheet 4.4 is a dateline questionnaire. Students should consider how far the criteria and information used in the questionnaire will help lead to a good match. How similar are these questions to those that a parent might ask in seeking a suitable partner for their child? They could then draw up their own questionnaire for daughters or sons to fill out, to help parents arrange a suitable marriage for them.

Pages 76–7
What happens at a Muslim wedding?

Muslim weddings vary a great deal from culture to culture and from family to family. Students must realise that there is no single form. However, Activity 1 enables students to identify the key features of a typical ceremony.

Worksheet 4.5 is a support worksheet for Activity 1, providing drawings about which students can make notes.

Worksheet 4.6 is a highly structured summary task for less able students. It could be used to structure work on the first three spreads of this investigation. Further support can be given by the teacher adding sentence starters or page references in the gaps. **NB** This letter is deliberately gender-free: the writer could be male or female.

Page 79
CHECKPOINT Contraception is not a big issue for Muslims, but the examination may ask questions about it.
Worksheet 4.7 is an extension or homework sheet to supplement the Checkpoint. It is an interview with a Muslim family planning advisor.

Islam in today's world Teacher's Resource Book

UNIT 4

Streetwatch: Balsall Heath

This features in the BBC series *Taking Issue*. The video can usefully support the decision-making activity. The teacher's notes which accompany the series are also useful.

This is a long investigation, and some interim review is necessary. So before you tackle divorce it is a good idea to pull together as many of the marriage strands as you can. **Worksheet 4.8** is a review task for use at the end of page 79. This may be used as an assessment task if required.

Pages 80–81
Divorce

This case study happened in Britain. It is useful for illustrating divorce but it is also useful to demonstrate the role of Shari'ah law in Britain today and how the Shari'ah can provide a structure of support for British Muslims. There is no single national organisation governing the British Muslim community. But the Islamic Shari'a Council is one of several Muslim legal councils that work independently in Britain, made up of scholars in Islamic law.

You may wonder about the interface between religious judgement and civil law. In the context of marriage and divorce, Muslims who are married in Britain must have their marriage registered at a civil ceremony for it to be legally recognised. Likewise divorce must be granted in the British courts of law to have legal status. However, a Shari'ah council can deal with marriage difficulties in a distinctively Muslim way and can support the believer in solving marriage problems.

4.3 Does Islam truly liberate women?

Perhaps the most commonly held stereotype of Islam is that it oppresses women. And perhaps the most common response to this, from Muslims themselves, is that in fact the opposite is true – Islam liberates women. This dichotomy has guided our choice of investigation heading. You may think that the truth lies somewhere between the two extremes, as indeed it so often does.

The main thrust of pages 84–8 is therefore about confronting stereotypes. It should be seen as something of a review investigation since the rest of the book is packed full of information about the role of women, and this can be referred to or re-used here. The investigations on the individual in society (1.5), ummah (4.1) and marriage (4.2) contain particularly relevant material.

Pages 84–5

Muslim men choose Muslim women whom they have found most inspiring. **Worksheet 4.9** supports the Activity. You could further extend this activity by allowing students to refer back to earlier investigations or, if they have a wide enough knowledge of Islam, they can refer to their own experience.

Pages 86–7

This spread addresses some common stereotypes. Students can judge for themselves what Islam teaches about women.

ROLE PLAY Worksheets 4.10 and **4.11** set up role plays on the issue of the role of women in Islam. Worksheet 4.10 focuses on work and dress, while 4.11 focuses on education and work. These role plays have been classroom trialled in a range of schools and have proved very powerful. In those of our own schools where Muslims are in the majority, they have worked particularly well, since the students bring their own knowledge and understanding to develop the role – essential for good role play – and have been very willing to express views that may not be their own. The worksheets can be adapted to different levels of experience (both of teachers and students). See the notes opposite.

Page 88
Mothers in Islam

This impassioned article may appear full of difficult language but it is less daunting once you realise how straightforward Ayesha's argument is – that motherhood is a demanding and rewarding career – and readers who disagree with the writer will probably find it more engaging than if they agreed. In mixed classes this piece will lead to stimulating class discussion. Here are some discussion starters:

- What are the advantages of doing as Ayesha says, and concentrating on motherhood first before developing a career?
- Is it necessary to force women to choose between motherhood and a fulfilling career?
- What does it mean to say women 'want it all'? Do you agree?
- Are women best suited to the role of child rearer?
- What is the role of the father in child rearing?
- Should the workplace adapt to allow men and women to share the role of parenthood? If so, how?

Worksheet 4.12 is an alternative to question 4, which invites students to write a letter in the role of a Muslim mother, in the spirit of Source F.

RUNNING THE ROLE PLAY This role play should last approximately 30 minutes. There are different strategies for running it, as follows.

Strategy One: Small groups
Experience level: Basic

1. As a class, read through the role-play situation together.
2. Divide the class into groups and give each group the character role-play cards.
3. Give participants 5 minutes to prepare and assign roles. One person from each group will play each character. Other participants will act as observers.
4. Run the role play for about 5 minutes. Then freeze the action and get other people from the group to take over the roles.
5. Debrief.

Strategy Two: Performed role play
Experience level: Medium
Steps 1–4 as above, then:

5. Ask one of the groups that had a particularly good role play to perform for the rest of the class.
6. Discuss issues.
7. Allow 5–10 minutes for participants to record their reactions to the issues.

Strategy Three: Staged role play
Experience level: Advanced
The key difference here is that the role-players are set up, and the outcome is fixed.
  Steps 1–4 as above, then:

5. Select a person from each group to play the relevant part in front of the whole class. Brief everyone on the outcome, and on their role, which is to be as obstructive as possible. The rest of the class observe.
6. Run the role play, but freeze it at regular intervals, and ask the rest of the class to suggest strategies to resolve the situation in the way you have already stated.
7. Students who are observing can also intervene by putting up their hand and directing the characters, or even by volunteering to take on the role themselves.
8. Discuss the issue afterwards.

UNIT 4

4.4 How do Muslims respond to racism?

Islamophobia

The Runnymede Commission's report on Islamophobia gained very significant press coverage and introduced the term to a wider public. It is also the natural starting point for investigating prejudice and discrimination.
CHECKPOINT Encourage students to use these terms correctly.

Page 89
ACTIVITY This invites students to conduct a piece of small-scale research which replicates a study conducted at the Kirklees Racial Equality Council. On page 4 you were advised to start collecting articles. If you haven't done so yet, then some speedy research will be required. You should look through the articles in advance to ensure that all students can find relevant data and not waste time.

Page 90
The Runnymede Commission on British Muslims

The full text of this report is available from the Runnymede Trust (see address list on page 15). It will be informative for teachers. It is a substantial report, but the helpful summaries at the end of each section may be accessible for the most able students.

Page 91
When approaching Activity B, teachers may find it helpful to discuss the eight points with the whole class and extract the core meanings. For example:

1 Using anti-Islamic language will be unacceptable.
2 There will be laws against religious discrimination.
3 British Muslims will be involved in all of British life.
4 People will accept the right of British Muslims to contribute to decision-making.
5 There will be state-funded Muslim schools but all other schools will provide for Muslim pupils.
6 Young British Muslims will be helped to develop an identity of their own.
7 Poverty among Muslims as well as in other communities in Britain will be tackled.
8 Employers will do all they can to stamp out discrimination. So will service providers such as hospitals. They will value Britain's cultural variety.

Worksheet 4.13 is a role play that raises issues of Islamophobia in a school context. It follows the same format as Worksheets 4.10 and 4.11, and the same strategies can be used (see page 71).

Page 92–5
Responding to racism

In this section Muslim ideas about how to tackle racism are presented through the experience of two very different Muslims.

Case study 1
This tells the story of Maqsood Ahmad, in his own words. He has already featured on pages 89–91. Maqsood grew up in Britain and cites many examples of his personal experience of racism, as well as the influence of Islam and his Muslim parents on his life. He is currently the Director of Kirklees Racial Equality Council.
QUESTIONS The essential prelude here is in-depth reading of the interview. You could encourage this in a variety of ways, for example by posing some quick quiz-style questions:

- Where was Maqsood born?
- What's his job?
- Where did he work before?
- How old are his children?

Followed by more interpretive questions:

- What does he think of the National Front?
- What does he think of segregation?

This will lead naturally into the questions, which are designed to probe the many possible responses to racism. If your students have never tackled this sort of 'zone of approval' activity before, make sure you talk it through in advance. The closer to Maqsood you place the card the more you are saying he approves it. There are many other ways of using this same device. You could repeat the activity for Malcolm X, before and after his consciousness-raising experience on Hajj.
    One of the objectives of Maqsood and other Muslims involved in the follow-up to the Runnymede report is that Muslims should be seen as a racial group (as are Jews or Sikhs) so that they have protection and redress under the Race Relations Act. This has significant problems attached, not least of these being the ethnic diversity of Islam. He alternatively suggests the adoption of Religious Discrimination Law as in Ireland. This forbids discrimination on the grounds of religious affiliation. A classroom discussion around these issues could be very productive:

a) What difficulties might each measure pose?
b) Why might Muslims want special legislation for their situation?
c) What alternative strategies might there be?

Pages 94–5
Case study 2
This tells a very different story. Malcolm X lived in the United States of America from 1925 to 1965. He too experienced racism from a very early age, but he reacted in a very different way.

UNIT 4

CHECKPOINT There are many 'outsider' tributes to the power of Islam in transcending racial boundaries. Here are two such tributes which we did not have room for in the Student's Book.

> No other society has such a record of success in uniting in an equality of status, of opportunity and endeavour, so many and so varied races of mankind. The great Muslim communities of Africa, India and Indonesia, perhaps also the small community in Japan, show that Islam, has still the power to reconcile apparently irreconcilable elements of race and tradition. If ever the opposition of the great societies of the East and West is to be replaced by co-operation, the mediation of Islam is an indispensable condition.
>
> *Whither Islam?* by H.A.R. Gibb

> The extinction of race consciousness between Muslims is one of the outstanding achievements of Islam and in the contemporary world there is, as it happens, a crying need for the propagation of this Islamic virtue.
>
> *Civilisation on Trial* by A.J. Toynbee

FOCUS TASK Students are invited to investigate the different factors, including Islam, that influenced the responses of Malcolm X and Maqsood to racism. This is a task of some depth, and you may feel that the issues need further probing. Most importantly students should recognise that different responses to racism are not just an issue of personality and upbringing but also of different histories and cultures. Arguably, although there are common features, the black experience of racism is not the same as the Asian experience, the American not the same as the British; the tenth generation of experiencing racism is not the same as the first. It might also be noted that anti-racist education in both the USA and Britain has moved on enormously in the four decades since the death of Malcom X, although many would still argue that it has not moved far enough.

Page 96

The first review task is in a different style from review tasks in earlier units, which have focused on exam-style questions. This is a much wider-ranging activity which, while it will prove a very worthwhile assessment opportunity, is not one that students will face in an exam.

Worksheet 4.14 is a 'Just a minute' quiz, where students must talk for one minute on a range of topics from the unit. **Worksheet 4.15** is an examination question for students to try, **4.16** is Qur'an quotation reference cards. Finally, **Worksheet 4.17** is a quick quiz which can be set as a pairs activity, as a class quiz or for homework.

Islam in today's world Teacher's Resource Book

WORKSHEET 4.1

The united community

What are the Muslims in Source A on pages 66–7 doing that helps build a sense of unity? Use what they are saying to help you.

Activity of a pilgrim on Hajj	How this helps build a sense of unity
All male pilgrims wear the same white clothes	
Worshipping Allah by circling the Ka'bah seven times with all the pilgrims (tawaf)	
Praying for Allah's forgiveness at Arafat	
Remembering the fight against evil by throwing stones at Mina	
Sharing the sacrificed meat with the poor on Id ul-Adha	

WORKSHEET 4.2

Life at the mosque

A new mosque has opened in your local area. Your class are helping the management committee to publicise the mosque. You are to make a series of posters. Each poster has a different target group. Each group in your class should design one poster for a group from this list:

- Young people 11–16
- Children 5–11
- Young adults 16–25
- Non-Muslims
- Parents
- A different group identified by you.

1 First read pages 68–9 carefully.
2 Make a list below of the features and activities shown in this mosque that would be of interest to your target group.
3 Plan the poster, thinking carefully about how you can make it attractive and informative, for example by using the right style and wording.
4 Create the poster, making sure each person in your group is actively involved. You should share out the tasks, for example:

- writing text that explains how the facilities of the mosque could be useful to the target group, Muslims and non-Muslims, who are part of the local community
- writing text that gives information about these facilities
- designing the main title and 'strap-line' (a punchy piece of text that will make people look at your poster)
- creating illustrations: drawing, using clipart, or cutting and pasting from magazines and newspapers.

Group: _____

Features/activities

WORKSHEET 4.3

*T*he ideal partner is . . .

A group of Muslim women in Nigeria were asked to make a list of the things they thought a Muslim woman should be looking for in a husband. They were asked to list them in order of importance. This is their list.

1 Cut out the qualities in the wish list below.
   a) In one pile put those qualities that you agree would be important in a lifelong partner. If there are other qualities that you think are more important than any of these qualities, add up to five others to your pile using the blank cards.
   b) In another pile put qualities you believe are unnecessary. Discuss reasons for your choices.
2 Place the qualities you want, in order of importance to you. Explain your order.
3 Discuss: Do you think it would be possible to find one person with all the qualities on your wish list? Explain your answer.
4 Why do you think some people are happy in lifelong relationships, but others are not?

Wish list for a husband

1 A pious Muslim	2 Truthfulness and honesty	3 A good leader
4 Justice and fairness	5 Love of children	6 Kindness and consideration
7 Readiness to consult his partner	8 Good manners	9 Chastity and good morals
10 Trustworthiness and reliability	11 Avoids quarrelling	12 Clean habits
13 Strength of mind and will	14 Gentleness	15 Generosity
16 A loving nature	17 Monogamous (content with one partner)	18 Sense of humour
19 Reasonableness	20 Firmness	21 Intelligence
22 Seriousness	23 Good looks	24 Physical strength
25 Wealth		

WORKSHEET 4.4

Dateline agency

Bright, active, lively, caring individuals sought for partnership vacancies.

We have thousands of opportunities like these to fill. Apply for a *free* compatibility test today.

For over 30 years Dateline has been responsible for many thousands of friendships, romances and happy marriages, all due to the quality of our matching system. Our unique and successful formula could easily be put to work for you. Simply complete the questionnaire below and send it to us today (along with three first class stamps) and you'll find out for yourself why it's never been a better time to join us. We will send you in the strictest confidence, entirely free of charge and with no obligation:

- The name and brief description of someone who could be your perfect partner.
- Our colour brochure with lots of information about seeking a partner and meeting people.
- A copy of our paperback book 'All You Need Is Love'

Call us anytime: **01869 351 525**

visit our website
www.dateline.uk.com

Dateline

Personal Information

Fill in or tick boxes where appropriate

| Mr | Ms | Mrs | Miss |

Surname | First Name

Address

Post Code

Tel. No. (optional)

Marital Status | Age
Single | Height
Divorced | Occupation
Widowed |
Separated | Religion

Build | **Attractiveness**
Slight | V.Attractive
Medium | Attractive
Large | Average

Your Personality

Affectionate		Fashionable	
Serious		Practical	
Considerate		Conventional	
Shy		Reliable	
Romantic		Adventurous	

Your Interests

Wining/Dining		Jazz/Folk music	
Pubs		Classical music	
Sports/Keep fit		Theatre/Arts	
Politics/History		Watching TV	
Reading		Smoking	
Travelling		Astrology	
Science/Tech		Children	
Cinema		Homemaking	
Pets/Animals		Gardening	
Pop music		Countryside	

I would like to meet someone between the ages of [ ] and [ ]

Dept. code **ESS 15**

© John Murray — Islam in today's world Teacher's Resource Book

WORKSHEET 4.5

Muslim marriage

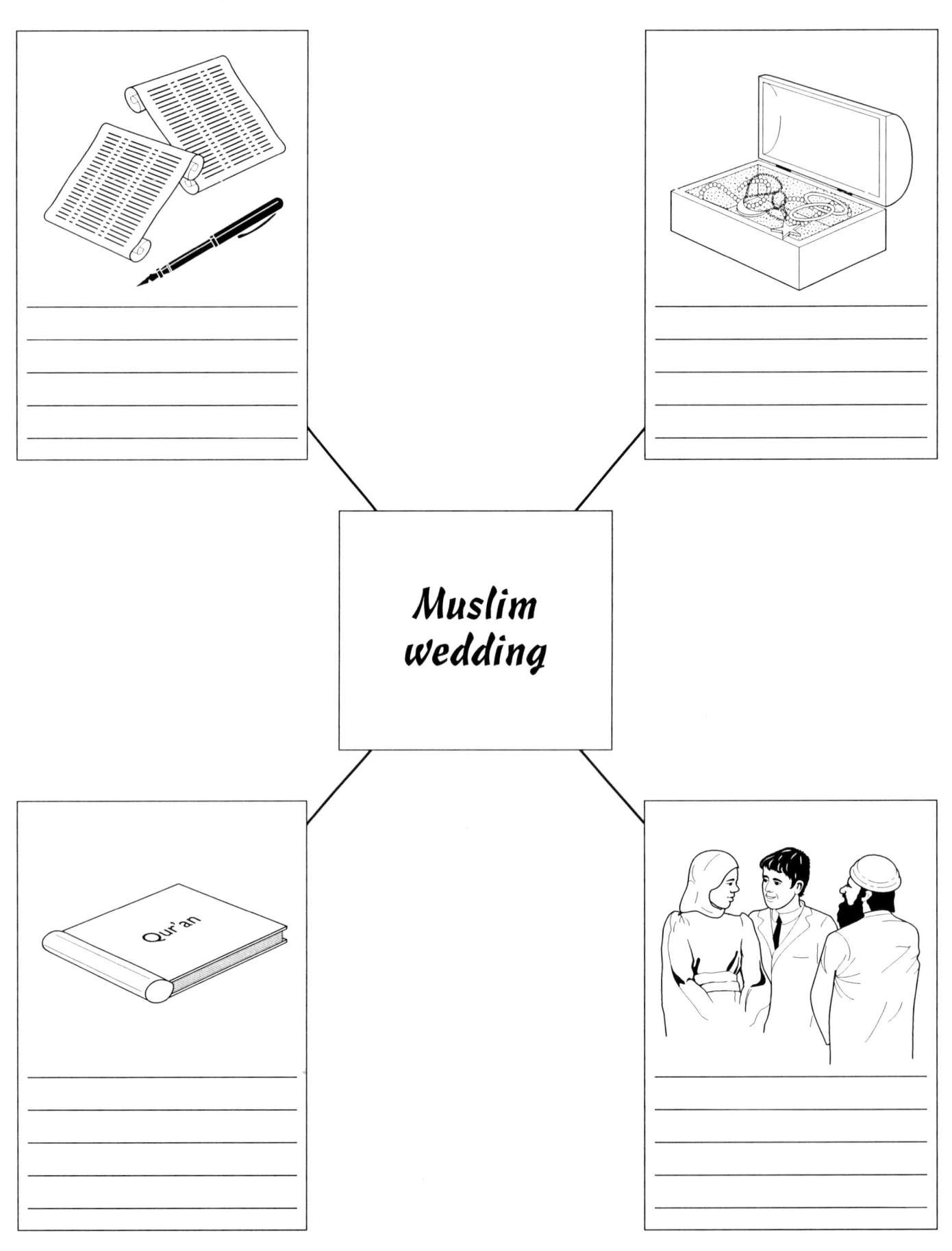

Muslim wedding

WORKSHEET 4.6

Marriage letter

Complete this letter to show what you now know about Muslim marriages.

Dear _____

I'm getting married! Yes me! Only six months to go and there is much to prepare. Since we are Muslims our preparations will include
_____
_____
_____
_____

I do hope that you will be able to come to the wedding. This is what will happen. First we will have to be married legally in a Registry Office, and then we can have our own religious ceremony. My parents have already hired a big hall for the wedding party.

When it come to the big day itself, one important event will be the signing of the nikah. The nikah is _____
_____

There will also be a reading of _____ and the giving of the mahr. This is _____
_____
_____

Enough of the practicalities. You will want to know all about who I am marrying! What a find! My parents have arranged the marriage for me. Our fathers have known each other at the mosque for years and we have met a few times before. My parents discussed it all with me. They chose carefully by _____
_____
_____

You may be surprised at me having an arranged marriage, as I know that you probably think it is wiser to fall in love first. Well, I am very happy. The marriage was not forced on me, and I am looking forward to getting to know _____ and making our marriage work. I think that arranged marriages work because _____
_____
_____

Getting married makes you think hard about your own values and your own religion. Marriage is so important to us Muslims because _____
_____
_____
_____

Lots of love from

© John Murray   *Islam in today's world Teacher's Resource Book*

WORKSHEET 4.7

'If Allah intends a child to be born then it will be born!'

Rukshana works at a family planning clinic in East London. What would she say about sex, contraception and Islam?

Deborah (D): Why did you decide to get involved in this type of work?

Rukshana (R): I grew up around here. Many of my school friends married very young and found that they were going to be a mother almost before they'd got used to being a wife. It was pretty obvious to me that some of them were more ready than others to become parents. Many of them were not prepared emotionally or physically for pregnancy and had a hard time coping with all the changes.

They had learnt about contraception at school, but assumed Muslims weren't allowed to use it. I decided to read up on the subject and found that some of the things parents had been telling their daughters were based more on cultural tradition than on religious teaching. I was already working for the Health Authority at that time, so I decided to get some training and transfer to this department.

D: Most young people are very shy about talking about sex. How do you overcome this problem?

R: We regularly visit schools around here, so I sometimes see groups of young women together. Also, there are lots of leaflets available, so people can get basic information about different methods of contraception without speaking to anyone. I speak to lots of people on the telephone too, which can be less threatening.

D: Do you discuss religion in all your interviews?

R: No. But Muslims don't separate religion from ordinary life, so when you are talking about sex and planning their families religion usually comes up. I never try to pretend I am an Islamic expert, but if they ask me, I will tell them what I have read.

D: What is the Muslim attitude to sex?

R: Sex is a gift from Allah. It's an important part of married life. Sex outside marriage is absolutely forbidden in Islam; Allah says in the Qur'an that if a person has not married they should not have sex. The Hadith tell us quite a lot about the Prophet Muhammad's attitude to sex and he provides a perfect example of the ideal husband. According to Islam, there are three main objectives to sex: to produce children, for physical satisfaction and as a way of demonstrating love and kindness between husband and wife.

D: So, how does contraception fit in with this way of life?

R: Most Muslims agree that contraception is allowed so that married couples can plan their family and ensure the health and well-being of all children in the family and of the mother herself. But the use of contraception requires the wife's consent in case it interferes with her enjoyment of sex or her desire to have a child.

D: Are some methods of contraception more acceptable to Muslims than others?

R: Oh yes. I think most Muslims feel that the more natural the method the better.

D: So is there agreement amongst Islamic experts?

R: No, Islam is just like other religions in that respect. People interpret the words of Allah and the Prophet in different ways. But I think that the advice in the Qur'an and Hadith is clear. For example, it says in surah 5.6, 'Allah does not wish to make difficulties for you,' and the Prophet did not forbid contraception when he knew that people were using it in his lifetime. I feel I am supported in my work by his example. In any case, no method of contraception is 100 per cent effective, so, 'If Allah intends a child to be born then it will be born!'

1 Rukshana says that no form of contraception is 100 per cent safe. Should couples only have sexual intercourse if they are prepared to support a baby if the woman became pregnant?
2 What do you think Rukshana means when she says that some of her friends 'were more ready than others to become parents'?
3 What are the advantages and disadvantages of getting information about contraception from:
   a) a book
   b) your parents
   c) a lesson at school
   d) a one-to-one session at a clinic
   e) your friends
   f) a telephone conversation with a family planning adviser?

WORKSHEET 4.8

Muslim marriage guide

You have been asked to compile an advice booklet for Muslim parents, to help them explain to their children why they should get married. It must be no more than four sides of A5 paper. It should be attractively presented and should include the following:

- A front cover, with a clear title for your booklet

- Some positive quotations on arranged marriages taken from page 74 of the Student's Book. Or you could add some of your own from your research.

- A list of qualities, like that on Worksheet 4.3.

- A section explaining why marriage is desirable for Muslims. You could use some of the references in the Student's Book, for example:

  Surah 4.23 – Why Muslims should marry

  Bukhari Hadith 67.42 – If you do not like your partner you do not have to marry them

  Bukhari Hadith 30.10 – Everyone who is able to marry should

  Hadith – A woman should only marry someone good enough for her.

- Some introductory aims for your booklet. These are often easier to write towards the end of planning your booklet.

- A section explaining the role of parents in choosing a marriage partner, and the reasons for this.

- Finally, include some suggestions of how to handle any problems that they might encounter.

Remember to be as concise as you can. Do not spend all of your time just doing the front cover design!

WORKSHEET 4.9

Women as role models

1. Read the text on pages 84–5 of the Student's Book.
2. Fill out the chart below to show:
   a) what the speaker admires about each woman
   b) qualities *you* see in this woman – use as many adjectives as you can.
3. Choose one woman and re-write her story, using your own research if possible, so that the story can be passed on to inspire a young Muslim.

	Why the speaker admires her	**What qualities you see in this woman**
Fatima		
Bint al-Huda		
Asiya		
Asma bint Abu-Bakr		
Nur Jehan		
Nasira		
Ali Miraj's mother		

WORKSHEET 4.10

Role play: Dressed for the job?

Situation

Burkett & Parry is a leading London West End marketing company. It has recently attracted an expanding customer base amongst Saudi Arabian businessmen. On visits to the Burkett & Parry offices in Oxford Street, comments have been made about the receptionist, a Moroccan woman, who does not wear hijab.

- Management feel it would be a good gesture to Saudi clients if the receptionist, Lamia, would 'cover up a bit'.
- Lamia feels this is unnecessary and against her personal preferences. Her bosses then formally request her to wear hijab.
- Lamia refuses.
- The bosses warn Lamia that she is breaking the terms of her contract, and arrange a formal disciplinary hearing.
- Lamia hastily joins a union.
- The disciplinary hearing will take place in 10 minutes' time.

Role card: Union official

Work out how you are going to approach the hearing. What will you say in Lamia's defence? What questions will you ask? What do you aim to achieve from the hearing?

The following questions should help your preparation:

- What are Lamia's grounds for objection?
- Has she got a case against her bosses?
- How much support is the union willing or able to give?
- To what extent do you sympathise with Lamia?
- What compromises, if any, do you think she should be prepared to make?

Role card: Burkett & Parry's Managing Director

Work out how you are going to approach the hearing. What will you say in your defence? What questions will you ask? What do you aim to achieve from the hearing?

The following questions should help your preparation:

- How important is it for you to win this battle with Lamia?
- What concessions, if any, are you prepared to make?
- Have you really got a right to insist she wears hijab?

Role card: Lamia

Work out how you are going to approach the hearing. What will you say in your defence? What questions will you ask? What do you aim to achieve from the hearing?

The following questions should help your preparation:

- How far are you prepared to fight this issue?
- Are you prepared to lose your job for your principles?
- Is the request reasonable? Doesn't the Qur'an state that all people, not just women, should dress modestly? In which case, isn't the bosses' request sexist?
- What concessions, if any, are you prepared to make?
- How supportive are your union, and how much help are they able to give you?

© John Murray   *Islam in today's world Teacher's Resource Book*

WORKSHEET 4.11

Role play: No place for a woman?

Situation

Shahanara is a student at a girls' school. After one year in the sixth form her predicted A Level grades are A in Religious Studies, B in English and C in History. The Head of Sixth Form is concerned that Shahanara has shown no interest in university prospectuses or the programme of careers talks. Shahanara explains to her that her family don't believe that a girl's education is important. They want to arrange a marriage for her with the son of a family friend.

Shahanara tells the Head of Sixth Form that she would like to go to university but that she loves her family very much and doesn't want to upset them. The Head of Sixth Form arranges a meeting with Shahanara, her father, mother and brother, to discuss the issue further.

The meeting will take place in 10 minutes' time.

Role card: Shahanara

Work out how you are going to approach the meeting. What will you say? What questions will you ask? What do you aim to achieve from the meeting?
The following questions should help your preparation:

- What are your family's anxieties?
- What is the basis of your argument for a chance to go to university?
- What concessions, if any, might your parents be prepared to make?
- You suspect that your elder brother is jealous of your academic success and is putting pressure on your parents about your marriage. How will you deal with this?
- How could you help the Head of Sixth Form to help you?

Role card: Head of Sixth Form

Work out how you are going to approach the meeting. What will you say? What questions will you ask? What do you aim to achieve from the meeting?
The following questions should help your preparation:

- What will be the basis of your argument?
- How can you argue for Shahanara's rights without alienating her parents?
- You understand from Shahanara that her brother may be a strong negative influence on her parents. How will you deal with this?
- What concessions, if any, do you think that Shahanara could reasonably make?
- How will you run the meeting?

Role card: Mother and father

Work out how you are going to approach the meeting. What will you say? What questions will you ask? What do you aim to achieve from the meeting?
The following questions should help your preparation:

- Why does Shahanara want to go to university so much?
- Will it benefit you in any way if you allow her to go?
- What will the rest of the family think if you allow her to go?
- Will she be safe?
- Do women need to be educated?

Role card: Brother

Work out how you are going to approach the meeting. What will you say? What questions will you ask? What do you aim to achieve from the meeting?
The following questions should help your preparation:

- Why has she done better than you at school?
- Do women need to be educated?
- Would this be setting a dangerous precedent?
- Will it benefit the family in any way if you allow her to go?
- Will you lose control over the family if she goes?

WORKSHEET 4.12

A Muslim mother

Complete this letter from a Muslim mother to her daughter on the birth of her first grandchild. You should read Source F on page 88 before you start, and include ideas from that article in your letter.

My dearest daughter

So now you are a mother yourself. I am so proud of you and am looking forward to seeing my first grandchild. The words of the adhan will already have been whispered in his ear and he will have been welcomed into the ummah – the family of Islam.

You also have now entered a group of special people – you are a mother. I know that women of your generation sometimes feel that the role of mother is not fulfilling. I can see why you may feel this way, because _____

_____

_____

But the Qur'an places motherhood at the highest level. Indeed, Muhammad ﷺ said _____

_____

_____

As a mother you have a special role to play in bringing up your child within the family of Islam. You will be expected to _____

_____

_____

There will be some difficult times (you were not always easy as a child!). You may find that you experience _____

_____

_____

But the rewards will far outweigh these problems and pains. You will find that you _____

_____

_____

I am looking forward to seeing you and your baby. I will pray for you, that you may fulfil your role with love and tender care.

Your mother

© John Murray   *Islam in today's world Teacher's Resource Book*

WORKSHEET 4.13

Role play: Too religious?

Situation

Wahid is a sixth form student at Valley High School, an 11–18 multi-faith comprehensive school. Recently the Headteacher has been very concerned about a group who have been distributing leaflets outside the school. Many students, including Wahid, are supportive of the group. They hold lunchtime prayer meetings within the school. The headteacher is concerned about this and keeps a close eye on them.

The Headteacher responds by breaking up the prayer meetings and discouraging all religious meetings within the school. He asks Wahid's form teacher, Ms Jones, to speak to Wahid about his 'extremist views' and his dress, which he believes is 'too religious' for a state school.

The meeting between Wahid and his form teacher will take place in 10 minutes' time.

Role card: Wahid

Work out how you are going to approach the meeting. What will you say? What questions will you ask? What do you aim to achieve from the meeting?

The following questions should help your preparation:

- How will you explain your dress and behaviour?
- What is the best way to approach your form teacher?
- What concessions, if any, are you prepared to make?
- Valley High is a school with excellent exam results. Are you prepared to leave the school over this issue?
- What support, if any, can you rely on from your parents? From the local community?

Role card: Ms Jones

You are in an awkward position. You have a great deal of sympathy with Wahid. You have a clause in your job contract, however, which means that the headteacher can direct you to do things. On the other hand, the school has an equal opportunities policy, and you believe the headteacher is contravening it.

Work out how you are going to approach the meeting. What will you say? What questions will you ask? What do you aim to achieve from the meeting?

The following questions should help your preparation:

- What is the best way to approach Wahid? How sincere is he?
- Can you carry out the headteacher's instructions without compromising your personal views?
- What concessions, if any, are you able to offer?
- Are you prepare to make a stand over this issue and risk a confrontation with the headteacher?
- What support, if any, can you rely on from inside and outside the school?

WORKSHEET 4.14

Just a minute: Relationships

You must talk for one minute about Muslim attitudes to *one* of the following topics.

1. Relationships matter!	7. Duties of husbands and wives	13. Islamophobia
2. Ummah	8. Contraception	14. Stereotypes
3. Life at the mosque	9. Divorce	15. Prejudice and discrimination
4. Extended families	10. Women in Islam	16. The Race Relations Act
5. Reasons to marry	11. Muslim mothers	17. Malcolm X
6. The ideal wedding	12. Racial equality	18. Muslims are Muslims first and members of a race second.

WORKSHEET 4.15

Examination practice: Relationships

Prejudice and discrimination

As you answer this question use only information on Islam.

a) Explain, using examples, the differences between prejudice and discrimination. (4)

b) What teaching is given about prejudice and discrimination in the sacred texts of **one** religious tradition? (5)

c) Describe how the teachings you have outlined in part **b)** are put into practice in this tradition with regard to:
   i) people of different races and
   ii) women. (6)

d) An Anglican bishop has argued that it is not always wrong to discriminate against other people; it depends on the circumstances. Do you agree? Give reasons for your answer, showing that you have thought about more than one point of view. (5)

NEAB (GCSE short course) RE Syllabus D, Paper 2 1997

WORKSHEET 4.16

Qur'an file cards: Relationships

Reference: Surah 17.23-4
Student's Book: Page 71
Name of surah: Al-Isra' (The Night Journey)
Summary: Be kind to your parents, do not be rude to them or send them away from you
Application: Relationships, parents, children

RELATIONSHIPS

Reference: Surah 4.128
Student's Book: Page 81
Name of surah: Al-Nisa' (The Women)
Summary: If things go wrong in a marriage, it is best to try to come to an agreement, but if you try and fail Allah will not punish you
Application: Relationships, marriage, divorce

RELATIONSHIPS

Reference: Surah 3.103
Student's Book: Page 114
Name of surah: Al-i'Imran (The Family of Imran)
Summary: All Muslims are brothers and must stand together in times of peace and war
Application: How individuals should behave in society; unity in Islam, jihad

RELATIONSHIPS

Reference: Surah 2.228-9
Student's Book: Pages 83/87
Name of surah: Al-Baqarah (The Heifer/Cow)
Summary: Explains the procedures for divorce and the rights of women
Application: Marriage, relationships, equal rights

RELATIONSHIPS

Reference: Surah 4.35
Student's Book: Page 82
Name of surah: Al-Nisa' (The Women)
Summary: If a couple are experiencing marital difficulties their families should try to help resolve them
Application: Relationships, marriage, divorce

RELATIONSHIPS

Reference: Surah 4.3
Student's Book: Page 75
Name of surah: Al-Nisa' (The Women)
Summary: A man is allowed up to four wives if he can treat them all fairly
Application: Relationships, marriage

RELATIONSHIPS

Reference: Surah 4.1
Student's Book: Page 77
Name of surah: Al-Nisa' (The Women)
Summary: Men and women were created from one soul; Allah guards over marriage
Application: Weddings, marriage

RELATIONSHIPS

Reference: Surah 30.21
Student's Book: Page 73
Name of surah: Al-Rum (The Romans)
Summary: Allah created partners for people for companionship
Application: Relationships, marriage

RELATIONSHIPS

© John Murray — *Islam in today's world Teacher's Resource Book*

WORKSHEET 4.17

End of Unit Quiz: Relationships

Test yourself or your neighbour with this quick quiz.

1. Define the word *ummah*.
2. State two ways in which Muslims promote the welfare of other Muslims within the ummah.
3. A Muslim can only pray in a mosque: true or false?
4. What is the *adhan* and why is it whispered in a newborn baby's ear?
5. What is the difference between an *extended* and a *nuclear* family?
6. State one teaching from the Qur'an on marriage.
7. What is an *arranged marriage*?
8. State one argument *for* and one *against* arranged marriages.
9. What is the maximum number of wives a Muslim man can have? What conditions are put upon him if he has more than one wife?
10. State two things that might happen as part of a Muslim wedding ceremony.
11. What is a *nikah*?
12. State one duty that a Muslim husband has towards his wife, and one duty that a Muslim wife has towards her husband.
13. What does the Qur'an say about sex before marriage?
14. Name two conditions of divorce in Islam.
15. How did Asma bint Abu Bakr help spread Islam?
16. State one reason given in the Qur'an why a Muslim woman should cover herself up when she goes out.
17. Define *Islamophobia*.
18. Is Islamophobia prejudice or discrimination?
19. How did the Hajj change the racist views of Malcolm X?
20. What was the purpose of the Constitution of Madinah?

UNIT 5
Global issues

Overview

This unit investigates three issues: wealth and poverty (5.1), the environment (5.2), and war and peace (5.3).

Most GCSE students will have a natural interest in these topics and may well feel deeply about issues such as the environment. There are also rich resources to be found almost every day in the print and TV media. Remember that investigation of the topics needs to go beyond the rather clichéd treatment characteristic of some media coverage, so that there can be realistic discussion, and balanced judgements can be reached. Remember too that this is RE – it is students' understanding of the religious perspective on such issues that is the main focus of this course, and that is what examiners are looking for. As in Units 3 and 4, students will have strongly-held views of their own on these moral issues – there may, for example, be committed vegetarians in the class, and they should be encouraged to articulate their views clearly. However, this unit is preparing students to answer examination questions about Islamic attitudes towards global issues, and it is vital that they explore these in detail as well as sharpening up their own views.

Starting strategies

This unit starts with a quotation from the Qur'an to provoke discussion of the issues. The key idea is that of guardianship or stewardship of a complex creation which has an impact on all global issues. This is reproduced in **Worksheet 5.1** with a poem by Olaf Skarsholt. Use this as a basis for class discussion. How do students feel about world issues? Are they just too overwhelming? What can we do?

Another way into the unit might be to bypass the textbook initially and to ask students to brainstorm issues which they think are affecting the planet today:

- Which problems to they think religion (generally) or Islam (specifically) might have a role in solving?
- Do they think that religion makes any of these problems worse?

This can then lead to the key issues in this unit.

Other resources

The media will provide very useful resources for all the issues covered by this unit.

It is important to follow up the specific Muslim teachings too. In the BBC series *Belief File*, programme one provides a useful exploration of zakah as one of the pillars of faith. Other videos to look at might include those from Muslim Aid, or the feature film *The Message*.

Local Muslims may well be willing to come in to talk about aspects of the unit. Muslim Aid itself has a group of speakers who work in different parts of the country. Teachers may contact this organisation, but should be aware that supporting GCSE teaching is not their organisation's main aim, and requests cannot always be satisfied.

5.1 How should Muslims use their money?

Use of wealth is an interesting issue for Muslims, since giving to others in need is obligatory as one of the pillars of faith. The investigation opens, then, with a spread on ways in which Muslims might give. It explains the three types of giving. It reminds us that zakah is not just about 2.5 per cent financial giving, but it includes other types of wealth too. This might be an interesting idea for students to ponder – if they consider their own possessions they may well be considered to be quite wealthy.

The second spread studies the work of Muslim Aid. This meets the criteria of specifications, which require students to be familiar with the work of 'a religious organisation which alleviates poverty'. There are other Muslim charities that might have been used – The Red Crescent, for example, and local charities may also come to mind in some parts of the country.

The final spread in this investigation is extension material on Muslim attitudes to the National Lottery. The issue of the National Lottery is one that taxes religious people of many persuasions, especially with the increasing dependence of small community groups on Lottery grants. This is a fertile area for investigation, as it highlights the problems of practising one's faith in modern, increasingly secularised, Britain.

Page 98

As a possible starter, the BBC video *Taking Issue* has a programme on wealth and poverty.

How to give

This spread is ideally used for class discussion. The opening explains the three types of giving laid down by the Qur'an.

An opening discussion activity might be to ask students to reflect on ways in which they (or other people) currently give to others in need:

- When did they last give to, or raise money for, a good cause?
- When did they last help a good cause other than by giving money?

Islam in today's world Teacher's Resource Book

UNIT 5

- How did they do it?
- Why did they do it?
- Did it help? Why do they think it helped (or not)?

And so on.

The one idea to draw out is that charity need not just be financial, and that many acts of charity are more about giving of time and talents. Students could consider how Muslim teachings might apply to their own giving. **Worksheet 5.2** enables them to do this. They complete a chart which records how they might follow Qur'anic teaching. Encourage students to be really down to earth in the column headed 'What can I do?' – examiners are looking for *real* things that people can do.

You could discuss what would happen if all the world gave zakah. Would there be no poverty or wealth? Or is poverty a fact of life? Would some people always slip through the net? Would inequality continue?

Page 99
Why do Muslims give?

Source C summarises teachings of Islam, a few of which it would be useful for students to be able to quote in the exam to support their statements about giving.

You could discuss the uses to which zakah may be put. It cannot be used to repair a mosque. The issue of spending on places of worship is an interesting one. You could collect a variety of pictures of mosques, from very simple ones (e.g. converted rooms) through to the famous and elaborate. Students could be asked to what extent it might be desirable for Muslims to have such highly decorated places of worship. Other questions might arise, such as whether the cost of decorating places of worship is more or less justifiable in countries where there is great poverty.

Pages 100–101
How does Muslim Aid fight poverty?

A preparatory activity might be to scour the media for 'needs' which might be analysed into categories, e.g. starvation, homelessness, refugees. They could also be classified by cause – natural disasters, self-inflicted, or human greed (compare pages 40–41).

Worksheet 5.3 draws out the difficulties faced by all charities in deciding who they will help. This could be a very valuable classroom activity. Set it up carefully. Ensure that students take it seriously. Prepare them to argue their cases. You could allow for appeals.

Worksheet 5.4 then encourages students to think about how Muslim Aid actually spends its money, and to discuss this. Draw out the distinction between long-term development aid (which enables people to become self-sufficient), and short-term emergency aid (which is just a stop-gap, to save lives, and which does not promote independence). The examiner will want to see that students know the difference, and that they have evaluated the two.

Page 101
FOCUS TASK This encourages students to show their understanding of the work of Muslim Aid, and the ways of giving, and reasons for doing so (pages 98–9), by preparing publicity materials. Remind them what is, and is not, appropriate in Muslim publicity. **Worksheet 5.5** supports this task.

Students may like to write to Muslim Aid for more up-to-date information about specific projects that interest them, or examples of leaflets to inspire them for the Focus Task. In this case we strongly recommend that just one student writes for the whole class, and a small donation is sent to cover costs.

Pages 102–3
Case study: Islam and the National Lottery

An alternative approach to issues surrounding the National Lottery might be to watch a recording of the televised Lottery draw. This could stimulate discussion about the charities supported, the 'hype' around it, and the attitudes of the people in the audience. Students might be asked to draw up a plan:

a) what they would do with the money if *they* won an £8 million jackpot
b) what they would do with the money (£8 million, say) that is allocated to good causes.

Then discuss whether this money really does help to make life better. **Worksheet 5.6** helps students to tackle the Focus Task on page 103. **Worksheet 5.7** is designed especially for less able students.

This spread makes a passing reference to the distinctive principles of Islamic banking. We have mentioned this again on page 106, but have not gone into this topic in depth since it is somewhat complex for this level. However, the whole area of Islamic finance is worth pursuing with students who have a reasonable grasp of economic concepts. A down-to-earth explanation can be found on the Internet at http://www.cwis.usc.edu/dept/MSA/economics/nbank1.html. An academic summary of Islamic attitudes to interest and ownership can be found in *Islam and Ecology,* ed. Fazlun Khalid, published by Cassell.

Note There is an interesting comparison to be made between the last line of source H and the title of the following investigation. Are they complementary or contradictory?

5.2 Live in this world as if you were going to live forever!

Young people take a passionate interest in care for the environment. A way into this topic might be a brief study of local environmental issues. For example, in RE one of our schools, students have explored the issue of local traffic problems in Cambridge: why there is a problem, and what might be done about it. Young people are often freer with their ideas than constrained older city planners! In the RE course this study is then linked to religious reasons for wanting to clean up the air. Worksheet 4.4 in *Christianity in today's world* Teacher's Resource Book is equally useful in this context as an issue-raiser.

Page 104

Sources A, B and C show environmental problems. They are deliberately ambiguous. There is no lead as to which problems are caused by human actions and which are 'natural'. A river bed might dry up through drought, damming, diversion, drainage; it might be part of an annual cycle. However, the point is for students to bring their own knowledge and even their own prejudices into these problems. The photos actually show:

a) a dried-up river bed (location unknown)
b) rubbish dumped at a scrap metal tip on the beach in the Seychelles
c) the effects of acid rain in Krkonose National Park in Poland.

Page 104

Masters or servants of Allah's creation?

This introduces the key concept of Khalifah. Students need to be aware of this in the examination and will need to explain for themselves the idea that Muslims are expected to care for the Earth, which is not their property but that of Allah. Students might consider other ways in which waste or harm might be caused, to add to the three examples given.

Worksheet 5.9 will help students to complete the Activity on page 104 without needing to copy out lots of material – this will free them to engage with the meaning of the texts.

Worksheet 5.9 is designed to help students to apply the teachings that they have been using. They are asked to produce two charters written by Muslims, which lay out what they feel are their responsibilities towards the creation, as well as the teaching on which they are based. Again, specific practical examples are required to get students thinking and to prepare them for the exam.

Pages 106–7

The work of IFEES

This relatively new organisation is committed to helping Muslims fulfil their role as Khalifah in this country. The written information on these pages is quite dense, and **Worksheet 5.10** is designed to help less able students to understand the work of IFEES. They put information into boxes summing up the main areas of work, in words, pictures, or a combination. The organisation itself is also worth contacting for further details if schools wish to develop this aspect of the unit. Again, remember it is a charity with limited resources.

Pages 108–9

The Oman case study emphasises how a government might be led by religious beliefs. This could lead to a discussion of how the British government might adapt its environmental policy in the light of religious beliefs.

Worksheet 5.11 helps students to complete the press release required by the Save As . . . task.

It is possible to discuss animal rights at this point. There was a video programme made by the BBC in 1986 called *Why Because* . . . The first programme, *All Creatures Great and Small*, has some interesting ideas to consider. Many animal rights groups are willing to come into schools to talk to students about their beliefs. This might be linked to PSE work.

The Assisi Declaration started a process that led most recently to the Ohito Declaration. This was ratified in 1995 and is a good example of cross-religion co-operation. Others will supersede that in future.

Worksheet 5.12 includes a copy of the Ohito Declaration, and asks more able students to consider it in detail. This is an interesting source to challenge your A* pupils! These two declarations might be a good context in which to discuss co-operation between religions: ask students to consider how this particular issue draws religions together.

Worksheet 5.13 will help students with the Focus Task on page 109.

Worksheet 5.13 can be used here as an alternative review task.

5.3 Is it ever right to fight?

FOCUS TASK Source A emphasises the basic Muslim concern for peace. This is at the root of Islam – that people should live together in peace. Yet we know that:

a) this is not how Islam is portrayed in the media
b) Muslims have got involved in conflicts of many sorts, as aggressors and as defenders.

This is an important investigation, therefore, in clarifying and separating Islamic teaching from the practices of supposedly Muslim political leaders.

Another way into this topic might be to ask students to describe (or to draw) their idea of perfect peace, and to define peace. They might then also try to discuss why this is not possible.

Alternatively, a video clip of a war or conflict in the news, together with the question: 'Would you expect a Muslim to fight in this war?' or the wider, 'Why are these people fighting?' might bring the message home.

Pages 110–11

The investigation starts with Muhammad ﷺ and his aim to bring peace in his own time. It then explains the Constitution of Madinah, which was an attempt to draw together the dissipated Arab tribes of Makkah and Madinah.

UNIT 5

It is from this that the concept of jihad as physical fighting has developed. Focus Task 1 on page 111 asks students to match principles used in establishing Madinah as one ummah, with the actual constitution. A copy of the constitution can be found on **Worksheet 5.14**.

Page 112
What does Islam teach about war?

It is very important that teachers help students to challenge the stereotype of Islam as warlike. This page might appear to confirm it. However, the Battle of Badr is an example of what Islam would deem a necessary battle. The radio report prepared for the Activity might be tape recorded and played back during revision lessons.

Page 113–14
What does 'jihad' really mean?

Jihad does *not* mean holy war. Jihad is a personal struggle against evil, which *may sometimes* involve armed defence of Islam and the community. It is important that students grasp this, and are not confused by the many times the term is used by the media and by political leaders.

Worksheet 5.15 will help students to complete the matching exercise in the Activity on page 114, and **Worksheets 5.16** and **5.17** enable students to explore whether Muslims might have described the Second World War and the Gulf War as jihad.

The blank chart on **Worksheet 5.17** might be used for any conflict that students may wish to explore.

The most interesting case study of all might be that of Palestine/Israel, if you have the time and resources to tackle this complex and shifting conflict in sufficient depth.

Worksheet 5.18 is an additional role-play activity based on various historical events that students will have come across in the Student's Book, or in their other studies. They are asked to see events first through their own eyes, and then through the eyes of Muslims applying Islamic principles. Try to ensure coverage of all the situations and give students the opportunity to watch and discuss other groups' role plays.

Pages 114–15

Worksheet 5.19 provides help for the Save As . . . task.

Worksheet 5.20 picks up on the idea of nuclear war. While it is not mentioned specifically in the syllabus, and is an issue that is possibly of less concern to young people today than it was in the 1980s, it is still an issue that is relevant while nuclear weapons exist. It may be worth spending a lesson investigating this topic and making suggestions as to a Muslim response. Local Muslims might be willing to come and talk about it.

Page 116
Peace-making in Palestine

This case study is pertinent to Christianity, Islam and Judaism. There is much material available on this project if you are interested in following this up.

Page 117
Global issues – Review task

This page is supported by various other review and revision tasks: **Worksheet 5.22** sets up a 'Just a minute' session based on various themes from the unit.
Worksheet 5.23 is an examination question which could be used as an assessment activity or for revision.
Worksheet 5.24 provides information on key passages relating to the global issues covered in this unit which it would be useful for students to know for the examination, and **Worksheet 5.25** is an end of unit quiz.

WORKSHEET 5.1

Global issues

If the Earth were only a
few feet in diameter, floating a few feet
above a field somewhere, people would come
from everywhere to marvel at it. People would walk
around it, marvelling at its big pools of water, its little pools,
and the water flowing between the pools. People would marvel at
the bumps on it, and the holes in it, and the different areas on it. And
they would marvel at the very thin layer of gas surrounding it and at the
water suspended in the gas. People would marvel at all the creatures walking
around the surface of the ball, and at the creatures in the water, and at the
green vegetation growing on the surface. The people would declare it as
sacred, because it was the only one, and they would protect it so that it
would not be hurt. The ball would be the greatest wonder known, and
people would come to pray to it, to be healed, to gain its knowledge,
to know its great beauty, and to defend it with their lives because
they would somehow know that their lives, their own
roundness, could be nothing without it. If the Earth
were only a few feet in diameter.

Olaf Skarsholt, New
Zealand, 1990

1 Read the poem by Olaf Skarsholt above and the quotation below, which is on pages 30–31 of the Student's Book.
2 What were your first impressions of each one?
3 Discuss similarities and differences in the meaning of each of them.

Imagine a palace with luxurious furniture, standing on a high mountain in thick forest. Suppose that a man found this house but could not find anybody nearby. Suppose that he thought:

- *that rocks from the mountain had collected themselves together to shape this splendid palace with its bedrooms, chambers and corridors;*
- *that the trees from the forest had split, of their own accord, into boards and formed themselves into doors and beds, seats and tables, each taking its place in the palace;*
- *that the fibres from the plants and the hair of the animals had, of their own accord, changed into embroidered cloth, carpets, pillows and cushions and dispersed about the rooms and settled onto the sofas and chairs;*
- *that the lamps and chandeliers had fallen from all directions and fixed themselves into the ceilings, singly and in groups;*

would you not conclude that this must be the reasoning of someone disturbed in his mind?

What, then, do you think of a palace whose ceiling is the sky, whose floor is the earth, whose pillars are the mountains, whose decoration is the plants and whose lamps are the stars, moon and sun? Is it not likely to direct the mind to a Shaping Creator, Everlasting, Self-Subsistent, who determined and guided?

Abridged from *the Creed of Islam* by
Dr Muhammad Abdullah Draz

WORKSHEET 5.2

Annual accounts

Muslims are expected to give of their time, talents and money, to those who are less well off than themselves. This voluntary giving is called sadaqah. Remind yourself about this by reading pages 98–9 of the Student's Book.

Complete this chart of the annual giving by a Muslim, either for yourself or for a fictional Muslim. (One idea has been completed for you.)

What do I have to offer?	Who is in need around me?	What can I do? (Be specific)	Muslim teaching I am following (Use the general ideas from page 98 and Source C on page 99)
• Time	• An elderly neighbour who is lonely	• Visit once a week and spend an hour talking with her	• Allah loves good deeds that are done regularly, even if they are little things

WORKSHEET 5.3 sheet 1

Hard decisions – giving to the needy

The Directors of the Islamic charitable organisation Muslim Aid are planning their action for the next three months. They have received a number of requests for help from around the world. These ten projects are described on sheet 2. Their total budget (including anticipated income) is £150,000 for these three months. Role play the decision-making process. The Directors must decide which projects they can support, and how. Do not forget to bear Islamic teachings in mind, and all that you have learnt in investigation 5.1 on wealth.

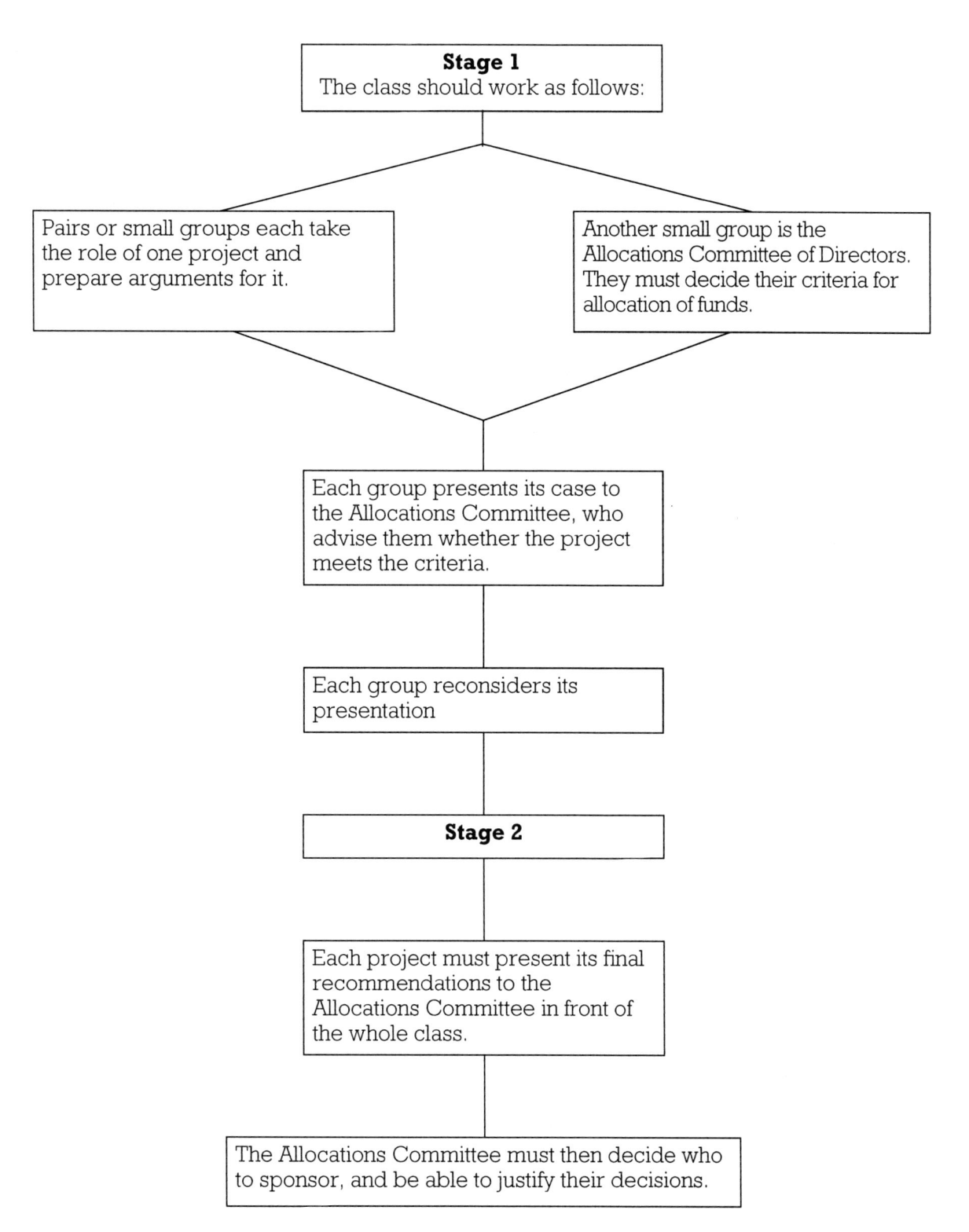

Stage 1
The class should work as follows:

- Pairs or small groups each take the role of one project and prepare arguments for it.
- Another small group is the Allocations Committee of Directors. They must decide their criteria for allocation of funds.

Each group presents its case to the Allocations Committee, who advise them whether the project meets the criteria.

Each group reconsiders its presentation

Stage 2

Each project must present its final recommendations to the Allocations Committee in front of the whole class.

The Allocations Committee must then decide who to sponsor, and be able to justify their decisions.

© John Murray *Islam in today's world Teacher's Resource Book*

WORKSHEET 5.3 sheet 2

Project 1
Continued fighting in Bosnia has left many children orphaned, and five orphanages have been hit by shelling, thus needing repair. To repair and extend these orphanages to cater for the increased numbers will cost £50,000.

Project 2
The people of a village in northern Palestine (pop. 3,000) are suffering from poor crops due to a lack of good irrigation facilities. A scheme to help them would cost £30,000.

Project 3
Healthcare in Africa is poor. Somalia desperately needs a hospital in the north of the country. To build, resource and staff such a scheme to provide free care for the 50,000 people of the region, will cost £150,000.

Project 4
In Australia many families are discarding family pets that they can no longer care for, or want. One home for such animals is so over-run that it needs to expand. This would cost £20,000.

Project 5
An emergency situation has arisen in Pakistan, where severe flooding has left thousands homeless. Basic aid in the form of food, clothing and tents will cost just under £100,000.

Project 6
There has been an increased number of requests from UK mosques needing aid for families for whom unemployment means that they are living below the breadline. £1,000 would help each family to get back on its feet. At least ten families are in real need.

Project 7
Unemployment also means that many people in Bangladesh are living on the breadline. Local Muslim partners would like to set up a skills-training scheme at an initial cost of £10,000, then £2,000 per 50 men and women supported.

Project 8
There is a real need to update publicity in Europe. Many Muslim families do not know enough about the work of Muslim Aid, and the charity would like to offer speakers who could go into schools to inform students about its work. This could cost £20,000.

Project 9
A cyclone has hit Sri Lanka. An estimated 3,000 people are homeless, and emergency materials are needed to build new temporary homes for them. Cost £30,000.

Project 10
The continued civil war in Rwanda means that there are now many orphans who are in homes, but who receive no schooling and so have little hope of a decent future. It will cost £180 a year to provide schooling and equipment for one child.

WORKSHEET 5.4

How Muslim Aid helps

1. Re-read pages 100–101 of the Student's Book which deals with how Muslim Aid helps to fight poverty.
2. On the diagram below, add notes around the edge to explain each aspect of Muslim Aid's work, and draw symbols or pictures to give examples of some of the projects helped.

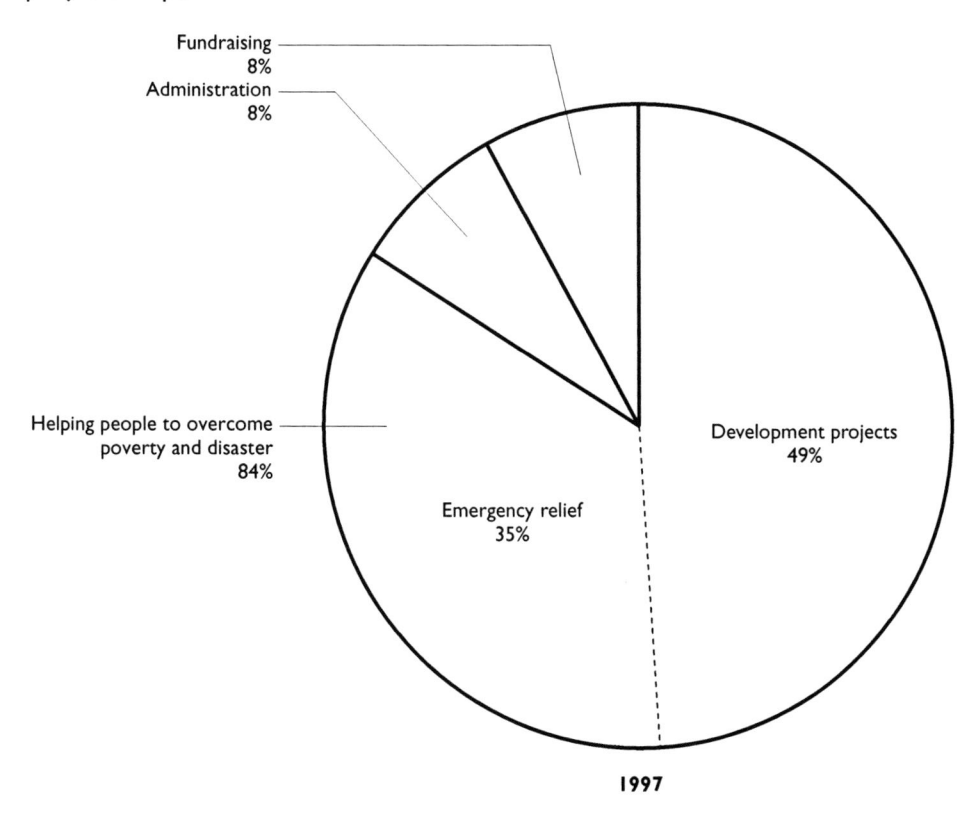

Pie chart (1997):
- Fundraising 8%
- Administration 8%
- Helping people to overcome poverty and disaster 84%
  - Emergency relief 35%
  - Development projects 49%

3. Do you think that the money is spent appropriately? Explain your answer.

_____
_____
_____

4. Devise a slogan for Muslim Aid which sums up how and why money is raised and spent. Write it below, or use it on your publicity material (see Focus Task on page 101).

_____

© John Murray *Islam in today's world Teacher's Resource Book*

WORKSHEET 5.5

Muslim Aid leaflet

This sheet gives you an example of a template from which you can complete the Focus Task on page 101 of the Student's Book. Your leaflet must encourage people to give to Muslim Aid. Think of how you can fill all the different boxes with images you have collected, or with information from the textbook. Plan your ideas in rough first so that you have enough space to include all the most important points.

MUSLIM AID Why you should give	Aims	Islamic teachings
	Muslim Aid's work	How Muslim Aid makes a difference to people's lives
Origins		

WORKSHEET 5.6

How can we fund our community centre?

This sheet is to help you think through the Focus Task on page 103 of the textbook. You are part of a committee drawing up plans for a new community centre in your town. This centre will cost many thousands of pounds. Some of this money will be raised from the local community, but the only source of a large grant is the National Lottery. Use the table below to help you and your committee to make a decision about whether or not to apply for a Lottery-funded grant.

Here are some questions to begin your discussion:

- Is the community centre really needed? Does your area have other needs that are more worthy of fundraising efforts?
- Could/should the local community raise the money through their own efforts over several years?
- Is the National Lottery a form of gambling? Is there any difference between the National Lottery and betting on a horse or in a casino?
- What does Islam teach about:
  a) gambling
  b) spending the profits of gambling?
- Is the community centre such a good cause that Allah may forgive the community for using money earned from gambling?
- Is lottery money 'tainted' money? Should it be refused by Muslims who fear the Day of Judgement?

Points in **favour** of applying for a grant:	Points **against** applying for a grant:

Our final decision:

WORKSHEET 5.7

It could be you – or should it be?

Use pages 102–3 of the Student's Book to help you complete this letter about whether Muslims should apply to the National Lottery for grant aid.

Dear Muslim brothers

I was interested to read about your dilemma over whether to apply for National Lottery funding for your new community centre.

Some Muslims argue that the National Lottery is almost the only source of grants today for building commuity centres. We all know the benefits of such centres. They provide _____

_____

_____

_____

However other Muslims feel that using Lottery money is wrong because

_____

_____

They would suggest you consider turning to _____

_____

as a means of raising the necessary money.

In the Qur'an, Allah says about temptation, that _____

_____

_____

We are also concerned about the sort of image that your action portrays, because _____

_____

_____

_____

In conclusion, my view is _____

_____

Your brother in Islam

WORKSHEET 5.8 sheet 1

Jigsaw

For this activity you will need three sets of jigsaw pieces, which are on three sheets:

1. Cut out the jigsaw pieces.
2. Now link a quotation with an instruction, and add your own example. Put them together in rows of three, as shown here.

instruction — quotation — example

1. It is He who has made you His agents …
   So He may test you in the way you use the gifts He has given you.
   Surah 6.165

2. If anyone plants a tree or sows a field and men, beasts or birds eat from it, he should consider it as a charity on his part.
   Hadith: Imam Ahmad, Musnad Volume IV

3. Live in this world as if you were going to live forever …
   Bukhari Hadith

4. O children of Adam! … eat and drink: but do not waste by being greedy, for Allah does not love wasters.
   Surah 7.31

5. There is not an animal that lives on Earth, nor a being that flies on its wings, which isn't living in communities like you.
   Surah 6.38

6. How can you reject the faith in Allah? …
   It is He who has created all things on Earth for you.
   Surah 2.28–9

7. Consider the water which you drink. Was it you that brought it down … or did We?
   If it was Our Will, We could make it salty.
   Why then do you not give thanks?
   Surah 56.68–70

8. Do Allah's work according to the pattern He set out for mankind: Let there be no change in the work planned by Allah.
   Surah 30.30

Set 1 are quotations from the Qur'an and Hadith.
Set 2 are explanations of the instructions in these quotations.
Set 3 are blank jigsaw pieces on which you should write one example of how each instruction might be followed.

© John Murray   *Islam in today's world Teacher's Resource Book*   103

WORKSHEET 5.8 sheet 2

Set 2 These are explanations of the instructions in the quotations in Set 1.

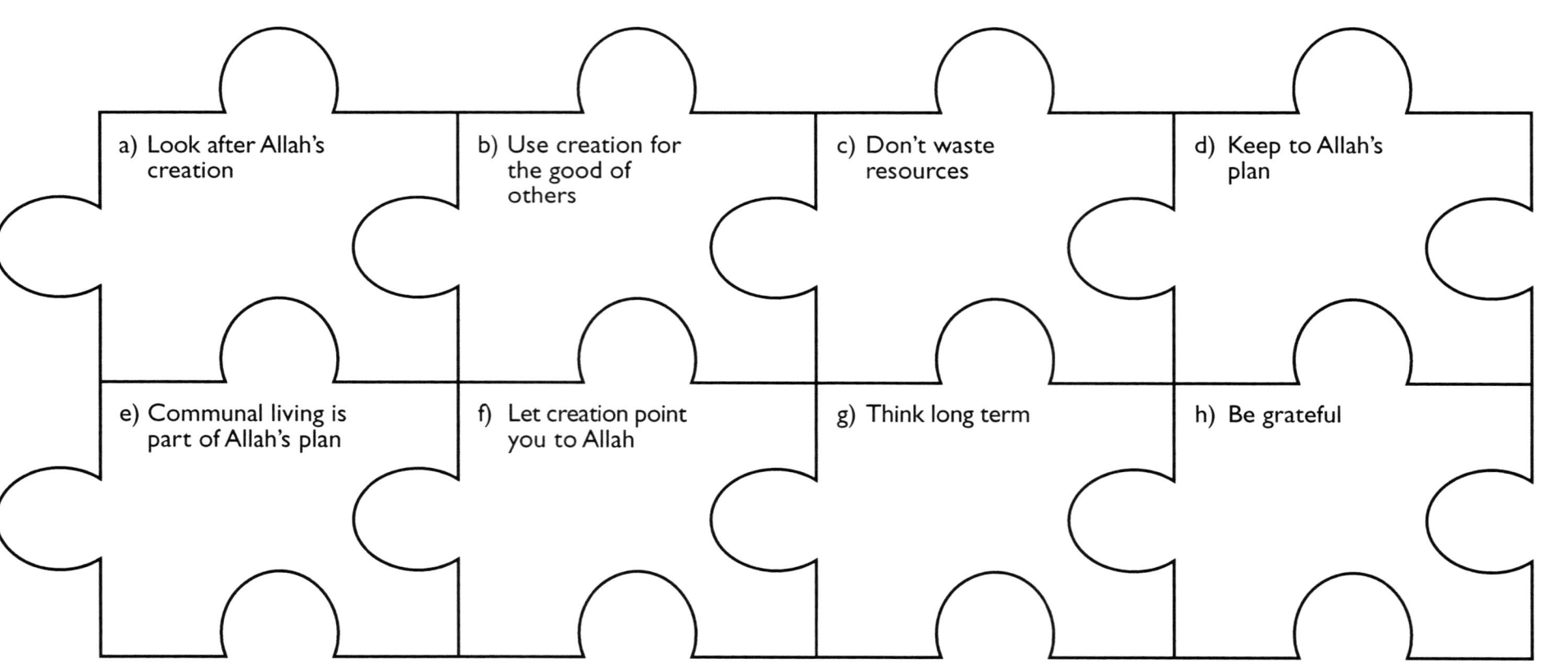

a) Look after Allah's creation

b) Use creation for the good of others

c) Don't waste resources

d) Keep to Allah's plan

e) Communal living is part of Allah's plan

f) Let creation point you to Allah

g) Think long term

h) Be grateful

WORKSHEET 5.8 sheet 3

Set 3 These are blank jigsaw pieces on which you should write one example of how each instruction in Set 2 might be followed.

WORKSHEET 5.9

A Muslim charter on the environment

Read the material on the environment in investigation 5.2. Now devise two charters (statements of intent) for Muslims that summarise their concern for Allah's creation, and their practical action in caring for it as Khalifah. One charter should be for the use of a local Muslim community, and the other for the governement in a Muslim state.

A charter from the Muslims of _____

In our holy book, the Qur'an, Allah states that
_____
_____
_____
_____

As a result all Muslims believe that
_____
_____
_____
_____
_____

Therefore we intend to take the following steps to improve our immediate environment
1 _____
2 _____
3 _____

We will check our progress by
_____
_____

and then we will celebrate our success by
_____
_____

It is vital that we carry out this pledge because
_____
_____
_____
_____

WORKSHEET 5.10

The work of IFEES

Use pages 106–7 of the Student's Book to research the work of IFEES. Then complete this sheet to sum up what it aims to do.

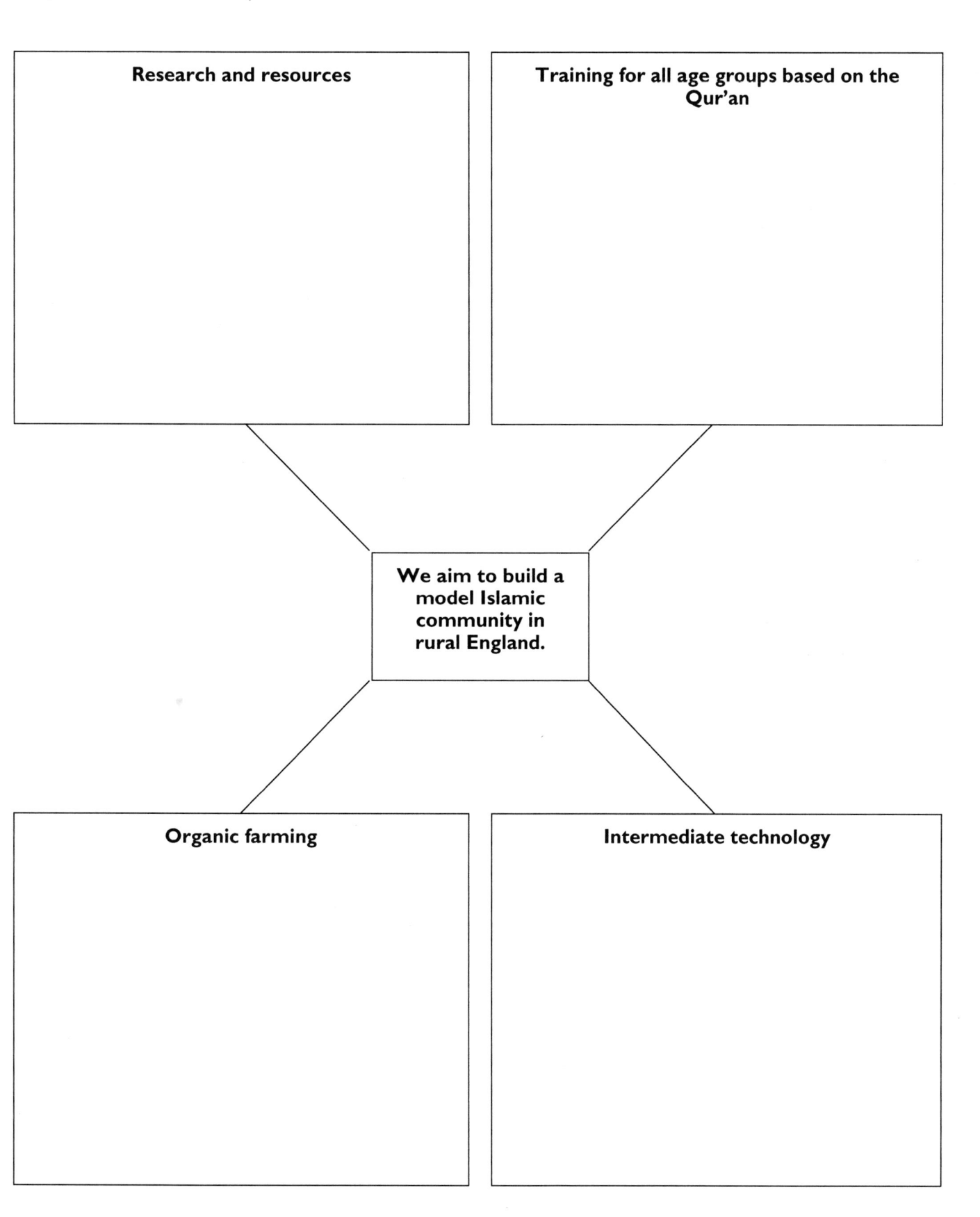

Research and resources	**Training for all age groups based on the Qur'an**

We aim to build a model Islamic community in rural England.

Organic farming	**Intermediate technology**

WORKSHEET 5.11

Press release!

This sheet is to help you write a press release for an Islamic news agency. You are to write a **150-word** press release celebrating the birth in 1982 of the first oryx calves to be born in the wild since the oryx became extinct.

Here is a list of key items to include:

- Sultan of Oman
- Arabian oryx
- In 1972 the oryx was declared extinct in the wild.
- In 1982, ten oryx were released into the wild, and later that year calves were born.

Refer to page 108 of the Student's Book.

PRESS RELEASE

WORKSHEET 5.12 sheet 1

The Ohito Declaration on Religions, Land and Conservation

Muslims contributed to the Assisi Declaration in 1986, as outlined in the Student's Book on page 109. They were also involved in formulating the Ohito Declaration nine years later. This declaration was put together by a conference of leaders of the world's religions, and representatives of the World Wide Fund for Nature and the International Consultancy for Religion, Education and Culture (ICOREC) meeting at Ohito in Japan. It was adopted at a summit on Religions and Conservation held at Windsor Castle, England, from 29 April to 3 May 1995. The declaration draws attention to current environmental issues and emphasises the role that religious communities should be playing in helping all people to respect the Earth and to preserve it for the future. It defines three aspects of the issue:

- Expressions of concern
- Spiritual principles
- Recommended courses of action.

1. In small groups, discuss these questions:
   a) Do you think that the expressions of concern are accurate, and fair?
   b) How would you explain these in more simple terms for young Muslim children?
2. Using the Student's Book, list three passages from the Qur'an which support the spiritual principles. Summarise the basic Muslim beliefs behind these ideas – you might refer to pages 104–9 of the Student's Book.

_____

_____

_____

3. List four specific actions which a local Muslim community, or children at a Muslim school, might actually *do* to follow the suggested courses of action.

_____

_____

_____

_____

4. On your own, make a poster explaining what the Ohito Declaration is. The poster is to go on the wall of a mosque, or in a Muslim school. You will need to think about its meaning for Muslims, and consider an appropriate means of conveying this.

© John Murray — *Islam in today's world Teacher's Resource Book*

WORKSHEET 5.12 sheet 2

The Ohito Declaration

EXPRESSIONS OF CONCERN

The health of the planet is being undermined by systemic breakdowns on several levels:
- faith communities are not taking effective action to affirm the bond between humankind and nature, and lack accountability in this regard;
- human systems continue to deteriorate, as evidenced by militarism, warfare, terrorism, refugee movement, violations of human rights, poverty, debt and continued domination by vested financial, economic and political interests;
- biological systems and resources are being eroded, as evidenced by the ongoing depletion, fragmentation and pollution of the natural systems.

Recognising the important parallels between cultural and biological diversity, we feel a special urgency with regard to the ongoing erosion of cultures and faith communities and their environmental traditions, including the knowledge of people living close to the land.

SPIRITUAL PRINCIPLES

As people of faith, we are called to respond to these concerns. We recognize that humanity as a whole must face these concerns together. Therefore we recommend these principles as a basis for appropriate environmental policy, legislation and programmes, understanding that they may be expressed differently in each faith community.

1. Religious beliefs and traditions call us to care for the earth.

2. For people of faith maintaining and sustaining environmental life systems is a religious responsibility.

3. Nature should be treated with respect and compassion, thus forming a basis for our sense of responsibility for conserving plants, animals, land, water, air and energy.

4. Environmental understanding is enhanced when people learn from the example of prophets and of nature itself.

5. Markets and trade arrangements should reflect the spiritual needs of people and their communities to ensure health, justice and harmony. Justice and equity principles of faith traditions should be used for maintaining and sustaining environmental life systems.

6. People of faith should give more emphasis to a higher quality of life in preference to a higher standard of living, recognising that greed and avarice are root causes of environmental degradation and human debasement.

7. All faiths should fully recognise and promote the role of women in environmental sustainability.

8. People of faith should be involved in the conservation and development process. Development of the environment must take better account of its effects on the community and its religious beliefs.

9. Faith communities should endorse multilateral consultation in a form that recognizes the value of local/indigenous wisdom and current scientific information.

10. In the context of faith perspective, emphasis should be given not only to the globalisation of human endeavours, but also to participatory community action.

RECOMMENDED COURSES OF ACTION

1. We call upon religious leaders to emphasise environmental issues within religious teaching; faith should be taught and practised as if nature mattered.

2. We call upon religious communities to commit themselves to sustainable practices and encourage community use of their land.

3. We call upon religious leaders to recognise the need for ongoing environmental education and training for themselves and all those engaged in religious instruction.

4. We call upon people of faith to promote environmental education within their community especially among their youth and children.

5. We call upon people of faith to implement individual, community and institutional action plans at local, national, and global levels that flow from their spiritual practices and where possible to work with other faith communities.

6. We call upon religious leaders and faith communities to pursue peacemaking as an essential component of conservation action.

7. We call upon religious leaders and communities to be actively involved in caring for the environment to sponsor sustainable food production and consumption.

8. We call upon people of faith to take up the challenge of instituting fair trading practices devoid of financial, economic and political exploitation.

9. We call upon the world's religious leaders and world institutions to establish and maintain a networking system that will encourage sustainable agriculture and environmental life systems.

10. We call upon faith communities to act immediately; to undertake self-review and auditing processes on conservation issues on a regular basis.

WORKSHEET 5.13 sheet 1

Muslim action on the environment

These sheets are to help you with the Focus Task on page 109 of the Student's Book.

1 Look at the statements below. Now complete an example to illustrate each level of action.
2 Write these examples or your own onto the ripple diagram on **sheet 2**.

Statements

Be aware that your actions have an impact on the environment.

Groups of people are more powerful than individuals.

Policy-makers have a responsibility to make people protect their environment.

Environmental issues do not recognise borders between countries.

Allah has appointed you His stewards over creation.

Examples

Instead of throwing all their rubbish in the bin, individuals should …

_____

Instead of complaining about the graffiti and rubbish in the streets, we could get together and …

_____

Instead of worrying about their own popularity, governments should make people …

_____

Instead of each country tackling their environmental problems alone, international organisations should …

_____

© John Murray   *Islam in today's world Teacher's Resource Book*

WORKSHEET 5.14 sheet 2

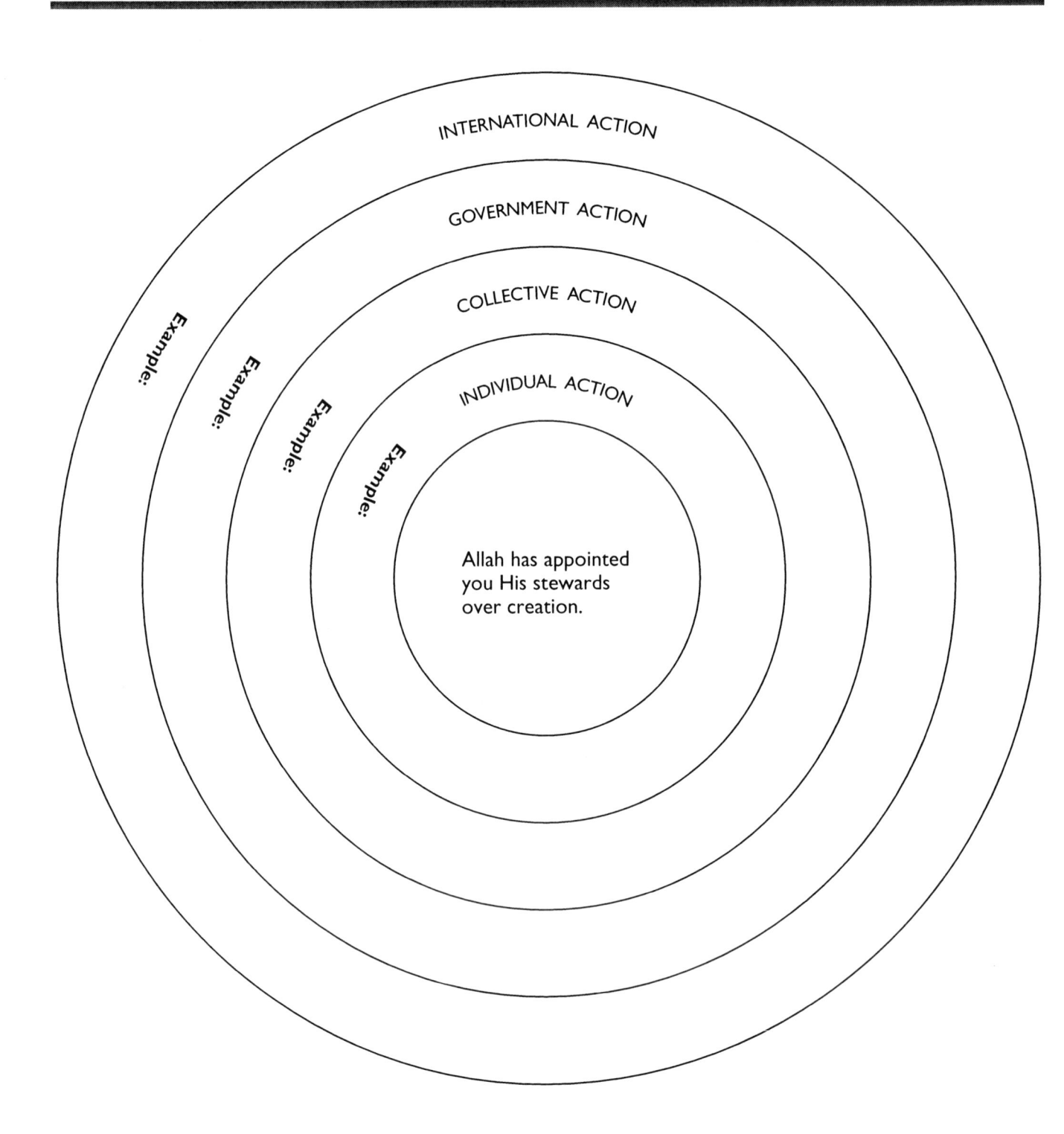

INTERNATIONAL ACTION

GOVERNMENT ACTION

COLLECTIVE ACTION

INDIVIDUAL ACTION

Example:

Example:

Example:

Example:

Allah has appointed you His stewards over creation.

WORKSHEET 5.14

Peace-making in Madinah

This sheet will help you complete the Focus Task on page 111.

An important aim of the document known as the Constitution of Madinah was to establish Madinah as one ummah – a community of believers living harmoniously together instead of as separate warring tribes.

Draw lines to show the connections between the ten points of the constitution on the left, and the six principles on the right.

1. The believers and the Muslims from Makkah and Madinah are all one ummah.

2. Any Jew who follows us has the same rights as anyone else in the ummah.

3. No believer is allowed to protect a member of the Quraysh or his wealth.

4. Any Jew who is with the believers shall share the expenses of the believers.

5. The Jews and the Muslims each have their own religion.

6. The Jews and the Muslims will help one another, consult one another and not fight.

7. Madinah is a place of sanctuary for the ummah.

8. Any disagreement which cannot be settled shall be referred to Allah and Allah's messenger, Muhammad ﷺ.

9. All members of the ummah shall join together and defend Madinah in case of attack.

10. Anyone who is told to stop fighting must do so in the interests of peace.

- All costs must be shared.
- All believers are equal, whatever their religion.
- People have the right to their own religion.
- Allah is the ruler of the ummah.
- People must try to settle problems peacefully instead of by fighting.
- The ummah will fight together to defend itself from outsiders.

© John Murray   *Islam in today's world Teacher's Resource Book*   113

WORKSHEET 5.15

When is it right for a Muslim to go to war?

This sheet is to help you complete Activity A on page 114 of the Student's Book.

1 Cut out the quotation cardss. Paste these into your book, leaving a space beside each one.
2 Cut out all the conditions for jihad and match each one with the correct quotation card. Then paste these into your book in the correct position.

Quotations

1 Three men refused to go out to battle with everyone else. They complained they had too many jobs to do, too many dates to harvest. Muhammad ﷺ responded firmly, refusing to speak to them and forbidding other Muslims to have anything to do with them.
   Hadith

6 And hold fast,
All together, by the Rope
Which Allah stretches out
For you, and be not divided
Among yourselves.
   Surah 3.103

2 Abu Bakr, the first Khalifah [successor to the Prophet] said, 'Do not be harsh on them; do not kill children, old men or women; do not cut down or burn palm trees, do not destroy fruit trees, do not slay a sheep or camel except for food. If you see people who have taken refuge in monasteries, let them be safe in their place of refuge.'
   Islam is the natural way by Abdul Wahid Hamid

3 If two parties among the Believers fall into a quarrel,
Make peace between them:
But if one of them goes too far against the other,
Then all of you must fight against the one that goes too far
Until they do what is expected of them by Allah.
   Surah 49.9

4 If people declare war against you, you may fight back, because you have been wronged by them –
Truly, Allah is Most Powerful for your aid
When you have been turned out of your home, which is not right,
The only reason this has happened to you is because you have publicly stated your belief in Allah.
   Surah 22.39–40

5 The Prophet said,
'Help your brother, whether he is the oppressor or the oppressed.' When they asked him how they
could help one who was an oppressor, he said, 'Restrain him from it.'
   Hadith

Conditions for jihad

- Every effort has been made to protect innocent civilian life, as well as plants and animals.

- All other ways of trying to settle a dispute have failed.

- They are not being allowed to practise their religion freely.

- It has been declared by a religious leader whose authority is accepted by the Muslim community. All able-bodied Muslim men must fight.

- The community is suffering under a tyrant; it is under attack and needs to restore its freedom.

WORKSHEET 5.16

Could the Second World War be called jihad?

There were a small number of Muslims living in Britain during the Second World War. Would they have been able to say that the country in which they lived was fighting a jihad?

Tests for jihad	Britain's war against Hitler's Germany in the Second World War	Jihad? ✓ or ✗ or ? and explanation
1 Every effort has been made to protect innocent civilian life, plants and animals.	1 There was intense bombing of German cities by British bombers. Hundreds of thousands of German civilians were killed. There was massive destruction of land and the environment.	
2 All other ways of trying to settle the dispute have been tried, and failed.	2 For four years previously there had been tense negotiations to try to settle the problem without a war. The British had allowed Hitler to get his own way to avoid a war.	
3 Muslims are not being allowed to practise their religion freely.	3 Religion was not allowed free expression in Nazi-controlled lands – notably Judaism, but all minority non-Christian groups were persecuted horribly by the Germans. All religions were allowed free expression in Britain, although there was increased emphasis on the Christian Church and its supportive role in war.	
4 A religious leader has declared war, with full agreement from the Muslim community. All able-bodied Muslim men are fighting.	4 War was declared and controlled by the democratically elected British Government.	
5 The community is suffering under a tyrant; it is under attack and needs to restore its freedom.	5 Hitler had already invaded or taken over one or two neighbouring countries in his attempts to gain more territory for Germany. He was tyrannical in his attempts to put down opposition. The war was fought to prevent him from invading other areas, and to free those under oppression.	

WORKSHEET 5.17 sheet 1

Could the Gulf War be called jihad?

The Gulf War took place in the Middle East in early 1991. On 2 August 1990 Iraq invaded Kuwait (a smaller country, rich in oilfields). After trying sanctions, a coalition of United Nations (UN) forces attacked Iraq (and Kuwait) on 16 January 1991. Iraq eventually withdrew from Kuwait on 3 March.

1 Read the first column of the table (on the next sheet), which lists the tests for jihad.
2 Cut out the following five statements about the Gulf War.
3 Paste them in the correct place in the second column of the table.
4 Fill in the third column to say whether you think each action was or was not jihad, and explain your view.

Religion did not enter into the war – except that Iraq was mainly Muslim and the UN forces nominally Christian.

The UN declared the war, with each member of the defence force being backed by their own government.

The UN imposed sanctions against Iraq after much discussion and attempts at settling the dispute by talking. A withdrawal from Kuwait was demanded by 15th January 1991 – this was not met.

Thousands of Iraqis and Kuwaitis were killed or injured, many of them civilians. The UN used laser-guided bombs and long-range missiles as well as conventional weapons; Iraq used chemical weapons and long-range missiles. There was huge destruction to the deserts and oilfields, and much loss of life, especially to seabirds and creatures.

It was felt necessary to defeat the dictatorship of Saddam Hussein of Iraq. The UN was defending the small, oil-rich country of Kuwait.

WORKSHEET 5.17 sheet 2

Could the Gulf War be called jihad?

Tests for jihad	The war against Iraq in the Gulf War	Jihad? ✔ or ✘ or ? and explanation
1 Every effort has been made to protect innocent civilian life, plants and animals.		
2 All other ways of trying to settle the dispute have been tried, and failed.		
3 Muslims are not being allowed to practise their religion freely.		
4 A religious leader has declared war, with full agreement from the Muslim community. All able-bodied Muslim men are fighting.		
5 The community is suffering under a tyrant; it is under attack and needs to restore its freedom.		

WORKSHEET 5.18

When is war acceptable to Muslims?

Work in small groups. For one of the following situations carry out two role plays:

A Sum up your own personal feelings and attitudes.
B Take the part of Muslims. Try to ensure that the views you express are accurate (use pages 112–15 of the Student's Book to help you).

You may wish to take on the roles of different characters in each situation.

---

1 The year is 624CE. You are living in Madinah and have been impressed by the way that the people of the city are now living together in peace. You have heard that Abu Sufyan and his army are heading for Madinah to fight against the city. Will you join Muhammad ﷺ's army to defend the city?

---

2 The year is 1948. You are living in Palestine and have witnessed the founding of the state of Israel. You see Palestinians being hounded out of their homes to make way for the Jews who are setting up new lives in the land following the atrocities of the Holocaust. How do you react?

---

3 The year is 1999. You live in Kosovo – once part of Yugoslavia. The whole area is in a state of turmoil. The Serb leader is following a policy of 'ethnic cleansing' and attempting to wipe out any non-Serbs. Many ethnic Albanians are being murdered and others are fleeing their homes in fear of their lives. You have been asked to join the guerrilla forces fighting against the Serbs. Will you?

---

4 The year is 1991. You live in Iraq. You are a journalist. UN forces have attacked your country in reprisal for its invasion of the small country of Kuwait. You have to report on the developing war. What stance will you take?

---

5 The year is 1096. You live in the city of Jerusalem. Christian armies from Europe have started to flood into the Holy Land to re-capture Jerusalem from what they are calling 'the Infidel'. You are required to fight to save your city. Do you?

WORKSHEET 5.19

What happens next?

This sheet is to help you with the Save As... activity on page 114 of the Student's Book. You must write a description about what happens next for **one** of the cases on page 115.

Case no. _____

A brief description of the situation:

Having read the situation we feel these Muslim teachings are useful to consider:

These teachings mean:

So in this situation the following should happen:

This hopefully will lead to this outcome:

© John Murray — Islam in today's world Teacher's Resource Book

WORKSHEET 5.20

What about nuclear war?

One concern that young people today have about the world of the future is whether it will even exist! The possibility of a nuclear war and all that such an event entails is frightening, as it could wipe out the Earth as we know it. In the 1970s and 1980s, nuclear weapons were developed in vast numbers and the arms race meant that many countries vied with each other to have the most powerful weapons. If nothing else, these acted as deterrents to other countries. Then in December 1988 the Presidents of the USA and the USSR (as it was then) signed an agreement that they would dispose of their nuclear weapons. That process slowly continues, but many of these weapons still exist, some owned by the most unlikely countries.

- Do you think that Muslims regard such weapons as acceptable?
- Is there a difference between owning them for deterrent purposes, and actually being prepared to use them?

Hold a class debate on the motion:

This house believes that true Muslims could not accept their country owning nuclear weapons.

Use the statements below to help you in your preparations. Try also to use Muslim teaching from the Student's Book pages 113–14.

• Nuclear war would result in the mass destruction of people, animals and the environment. That would break one of the conditions of jihad.	• We are not caring for other people if we destroy them with nuclear weapons – unless we are defending our right to practise our religion.
• It is wrong to spend vast amounts of money on weapons that are simply defensive – this is an abuse of wealth and poor stewardship of Allah's gifts.	• We should be defending others, not fighting against them. Muhammad ﷺ told us to: 'Help your brother, whether he is the oppressor or the oppressed' (Surah 3.103).
• We make our own country vulnerable by having weapons.	• Owning such weapons encourages their use, rather than trying to settle disputes peacefully first.
• There is no harm in holding weapons as a deterrent – we are protecting the vulnerable in society. This is an example of ummah.	• The threat of such weapons is the only thing that some tyrants will 'listen to'.
• Our country should set an example to others and disarm – they will follow.	• Unfortunately we cannot just disinvent these weapons – we need to find ways of making them safe instead.
• It is naive to believe that people are selfless these days – others will not follow any example of disarmament.	• Who knows which countries will keep their weapons if we all claim to disarm?
• There could be a mistake and the weapons might be used.	

Islam in today's world Teacher's Resource Book © John Murray

WORKSHEET 5.21

Just a minute: Global issues

Note to teachers
1. Copy and cut out the statements on this sheet.
2. Give each student one of the statements.
3. Ask the students to prepare notes that will enable them to speak in support of their statement for at least one minute, with no pauses! They should try to include relevant Muslim teachings or ideas. If they disagree with the statement it should not matter – they can express their own views afterwards.

1. Muslims should not be rich.	13. Muslims must not waste the resources of the Earth.
2. Muslims should not be rich if they do not share their wealth.	14. 'Live in this world as if you were going to live forever!' (Bukhari Hadith)
3. Allah commands Muslims to give to those in need.	15. The work of IFEES is important.
4. Zakah is very important to Muslims.	16. Individuals can be Khalifah in many ways.
5. Sadaqah should be practised by Muslims every day.	17. Operation Oryx is an example to everyone.
6. Muslims should give to Muslim Aid.	18. The Assisi Declaration shows that religion has a role to play in protecting the environment.
7. 'The deeds most loved by Allah are those that are done regularly even though they may be small' (Bukhari Hadith 29.40).	19. Animals have as much right to respect as humans.
8. The work of Muslim Aid makes a difference.	20. Jihad is not possible today.
9. Muslims should only give to Muslim charities.	21. Despite modern warfare, it is still possible to have jihad.
10. A Muslim should not buy a lottery ticket.	22. Muslims must not be pacifists.
11. Muslims must care for Allah's creation.	23. Muhammad ﷺ was a leader in peace and war.
12. It is not only Muslims who should care for the creation.	24. The Open House Project in Palestine shows how religion can play a role in peace-making.

© John Murray — *Islam in today's world Teacher's Resource Book*

WORKSHEET 5.22

Examination practice: Global issues

The natural world

As you answer this question use only information on Islam.

a) Outline the teachings of **one** religious tradition about the relationship between human beings and animals. (5)

b) Why are some religious believers vegetarians? (4)

c) Describe **two** ways in which **one** religious tradition is working to help take care of the planet. In your answer state clearly the religious or moral reasons for their views. (6)

d) 'How I live is up to me, it doesn't affect anyone or anything else.' Do you agree? Give reasons for your answer, showing that you have thought about more than one point of view. (5)

WORKSHEET 5.23

Qur'an file cards: Global issues

Reference: Surah 2.164
Student's Book: Page 97
Name of surah: Al-Baqarah (The Heifer/Cow)
Summary: Signs of Allah may be seen in His creation.
Application: Creation, responsibility for the environment, proof of Allah

---

Reference: Surah 49.9
Student's Book: Page 114
Name of surah: Al-Hujurat (The Chambers)
Summary: If there is an argument between two people or groups, help them to settle it. But if one of them goes too far then everyone must fight against them
Application: Resolving conflict

Reference: Surah 6.165
Student's Book: Page 105
Name of surah: Al-An'am (The Cattle)
Summary: Allah is testing human beings by giving them responsibility for His creation
Application: Responsibility

Reference: Surah 22.39–40
Student's Book: Page 114
Name of surah: Al-Hajj (The Pilgrimage)
Summary: Fighting is acceptable only in defence of Islam
Application: Resolving conflict

Reference: Surah 6.38
Student's Book: Page 105
Name of surah: Al-An'am (The Cattle)
Summary: All creatures live together naturally in groups
Application: Relationships, animals, the environment

Reference: Surah 3.92
Student's Book: Page 22
Name of surah: Al-i'Imran – The Family of Imran
Summary: A person cannot say they are a true Muslim until they are prepared to give what is valuable to them
Application: The responsibility of one Muslim to another. The different ways in which Muslims can help each other

---

Reference: Surah 56.68–70
Student's Book: Page 105
Name of surah: Al-Waqi'ah (The Inevitable)
Summary: Give thanks for the world; do not take it for granted
Application: Creation, environment

WORKSHEET 5.24

End of Unit Quiz: Global issues

Test yourself or your neighbour with this quick quiz.

1. True or false? All Muslims must give generously.
2. Name two things that *zakah* can be spent on.
3. What is the Muslim word for a good deed?
4. When is Zakat-ul-Fitr paid?
5. What is *Muslim Aid*?
6. In what way is Muslim Aid unique?
7. Explain two things that Muslim Aid does.
8. Explain why Muslim Aid exists.
9. How does Muslim Aid raise its funds?
10. Explain why a Muslim should not play the National Lottery.
11. What does the word *Khalifah* mean?
12. State two global problems.
13. What does the Qur'an teach about wealth?
14. What is *long-term aid*?
15. Give one reason why Muslims should be involved in caring for the world.
16. State one example of Muslims tackling an environmental problem.
17. What is *jihad*?
18. State one teaching from the Qur'an on war and violence.
19. State two arguments that a Muslim might give *for* the use of violence.
20. State two arguments that a Muslim might give *against* the use of violence.